THEOLOGY AS INTERDISCIPLINARY INQUIRY

Theology as Interdisciplinary Inquiry

Learning with and from the Natural and Human Sciences

Edited by

Robin W. Lovin *&* Joshua Mauldin

WILLIAM. B. EERDMANS PUBLISHING COMPANY
GRAND RAPIDS, MICHIGAN

Wm. B. Eerdmans Publishing Co.
2140 Oak Industrial Drive N.E., Grand Rapids, Michigan 49505
www.eerdmans.com

23 22 21 20 19 18 17   1 2 3 4 5 6 7

ISBN 978-0-8028-7388-0

Library of Congress Cataloging-in-Publication Data

Names: Lovin, Robin W., editor. | Mauldin, Joshua, 1983– editor.
Title: Theology as interdisciplinary inquiry : learning with and from the natural
    and human sciences / edited by Robin W. Lovin & Joshua Mauldin.
Description: Grand Rapids, Michigan : William. B. Eerdmans Publishing
    Company, [2017] | Includes bibliographical references and index.
Identifiers: LCCN 2016049847 | ISBN 9780802873880 (pbk. : alk. paper)
Subjects: LCSH: Theology. | Theological anthropology--Christianity. | Religion
    and science.
Classification: LCC BR118 .T4827 2017 | DDC 230.01—dc23
    LC record available at https://lccn.loc.gov/2016049847

In memory of Jack Templeton

Contents

Foreword, by William Storrar   ix

Acknowledgments   xi

Introduction: Theology as Interdisciplinary Inquiry   xiii
The Virtues of Humility and Hope
    Robin Lovin, Peter Danchin, Agustín Fuentes,
    Friederike Nüssel, and Stephen Pope

1. **Looking at Humans through the Lens of Deep History**   1
A Transdisciplinary Approach to Theology
and Evolutionary Anthropology
    Celia Deane-Drummond

2. **The Moral Life and the Structures of Rational Selves**   23
Theology and Science on *Habitus, Imitatio,* and the
Valuation of Self and Other
    Michael Spezio

3. **In the Divine (Mental) Image**   50
Theological Anthropology and the
Structures of Cognition
    Colleen Shantz

CONTENTS

4. Nicholas of Cusa's Mystical Theology in
   Theological and Scientific Perspective   68
   Textuality, Intersubjectivity, Transformation
       Andrea Hollingsworth

5. Religious Persecution and Religious Freedom   91
   The Witness of Russia's New Martyrs and Holy Elders
       John P. Burgess

6. Law, Theology, and Aesthetics   112
   Identifying the Sources of Authority
       Mary Ellen O'Connell

   Conclusion: A Collaborative Manner of
   Theological Reflection   132
       Douglas F. Ottati

   Contributors   161

   Center of Theological Inquiry Research Fellows,
   2012–2015   163

   Index   165

Foreword

The Center of Theological Inquiry is an independent research institution in Princeton, New Jersey. Our mission is to bring theology into dialogue with other disciplines on questions of mutual concern. To that end, we convene leading thinkers in an interdisciplinary research environment where theology makes an impact on global concerns, and we share those discoveries to change the way people think and act.

This book shares the wisdom we gained about the nature and practice of interdisciplinary theological inquiry in a research project led by Robin Lovin and Friederike Nüssel. From 2012 to 2015 the Center convened resident research teams of theologians, scientists, and legal scholars to pursue yearlong inquiries on three distinct but related topics of global concern: human nature, human flourishing, and human society. The Center wishes to thank the researchers for their participation, the John Templeton Foundation for its sponsorship, and Robin Lovin and Joshua Mauldin for their editorial work on this volume.

John Calvin memorably stated that our wisdom consists almost entirely of two parts: the knowledge of God and of ourselves. By pursuing three interdisciplinary inquiries on what it means to be human, drawing on the disciplines of anthropology, psychology, and law, the Center has gained a deeper understanding of the discipline that concerns itself with the knowledge of God—theology. More than that, we have come to appreciate afresh the insight of the Center's founder, James McCord, that theological inquiry is not the work of theology alone. It is an endeavor that requires us to think across all boundaries of human inquiry in the sciences and humanities, law and theology.

Theology as Interdisciplinary Inquiry is therefore a fruit of the Center's mission to foster theology's interdisciplinary conversation on global concerns. As the opening essay reminds us, such thinking across borders calls for humility and hope. In all humility, we hope this volume may help theologians and scholars in other disciplines to think and act together for the global good.

WILLIAM STORRAR
Director
Center of Theological Inquiry

Acknowledgments

This volume draws on the collaboration of thirty-nine scholars in theology, the sciences, humanities, and law who participated in the Center of Theological Inquiry (CTI) research project "New Approaches in Theological Inquiry," made possible by a grant from the John Templeton Foundation. The project comprised three interdisciplinary theological inquiries: on evolution and human nature (2012–2013), on religious experience and moral identity (2013–2014), and on law and religious freedom (2014–2015). The members of CTI in this project are listed on pages 163–64. The six scholars whose essays make up the body of this volume exemplify the research done in the three inquiries. We appreciate their scholarship, creativity, and continuing interest in the work of CTI, along with the work of their colleagues from the inquiries who coauthored the introductory essay and Professor Douglas Ottati, who authored the concluding essay, which reflects on the theological work of the three inquiries. We also thank Isaac Kim, a graduate student at Princeton Theological Seminary, for his careful work in preparing the manuscript for publication.

Publishing a volume that breaks new ground in theological method requires an exceptional publisher. CTI has been fortunate to enjoy a long association with William B. Eerdmans Publishing Company in publishing its research. *Theology as Interdisciplinary Inquiry* shares in that good fortune. In particular, we want to record our gratitude to Jon Pott, who commissioned this volume for publication as one of his final acts as editor-in-chief at Eerdmans, and to his successor, James Ernest, who has been equally supportive in bringing it to a wider readership of scholars and students interested in interdisciplinary theological inquiry.

Partnerships have been a key element in the success of the interdisciplinary research project that undergirds this volume. On behalf of CTI, we thank the following institutions and colleagues for their collaboration: Kim Lane Scheppele and the Program in Law and Public Affairs, Princeton University; Robert Wuthnow and the Center for the Study of Religion, Princeton University; Robert Gibbs, director, Jackman Humanities Institute, University of Toronto; Holmes Rolston; Niels Gregersen; Angela Creager; Jennifer Herdt; Linda Woodhead; Melvin Konner; Sarah Coakley; Simon Conway Morris; Wentzel van Huyssteen; Paul Bloom; Jean Porter; William Hurlbut; Werner Jeanrond; Jeremy Waldron; Cathleen Kaveny; Shaun Casey; John Witte; Nigel Biggar; David Hollenbach; Rudolf von Sinner, Brazil; Ernst Conradie, Danie Veldsman, Johan Buitendag, South Africa; Zhibin Xie, China; and David Tombs, New Zealand.

This volume began its life in a conversation with Michael Murray, a senior staff member at the John Templeton Foundation. That conversation led to a grant proposal that was approved by the foundation's president, the late Dr. Jack Templeton. The proposal included a commitment to publishing a capstone book of essays on the project. It is fitting, then, that in thanking Michael Murray, and his colleague Andrew Rick-Miller, for their guidance to CTI on behalf of the Templeton Foundation, we dedicate this volume to the memory of Jack Templeton in gratitude for his commitment to thinking across boundaries.

INTRODUCTION

Theology as Interdisciplinary Inquiry

The Virtues of Humility and Hope

ROBIN LOVIN, PETER DANCHIN, AGUSTÍN FUENTES,
FRIEDERIKE NÜSSEL, AND STEPHEN POPE

Something unusual is happening when a theologian interested in mysticism asks a neuroscientist how she should interpret a medieval text. Something perhaps even less expected occurs when an evolutionary anthropologist asks a historian of religion for help in understanding how social cooperation affects the way the human species re-creates its evolutionary niche. New lines of investigation are also opened when a legal scholar and a theologian both take an interest in aesthetics in an effort to understand what the authority of law might share with religious awe. Such unlikely conversations are happening with increasing frequency, not only in chance encounters between colleagues, but in structured interdisciplinary discussions that draw together advances in several fields and set directions for future research.

Theologians, in particular, have been active participants in these conversations. The beginnings of many new currents in theology can be traced to theologians who responded to hard questions about the origins of life, the social role of religion, and the psychology of belief, but their work would not have been possible without engagement with gender studies, sociology, psychology, medicine, natural sciences, political theory, and critical theory. Recent years have seen remarkable treatments that focus different disciplinary perspectives on perennial human questions. Wentzel van Huyssteen has worked out the points of contact between scientific inquiry and religious understanding of human uniqueness. Jeremy Waldron argues for historical and conceptual connections between the modern conception of human rights and religious ideas of human dignity. Melvin Konner presents an account of childhood built on a detailed interweaving of evolutionary biology, psychology, and spirituality.[1]

The aim of this book is to call attention to this growing body of work and to encourage more general theological reflection on the possibilities for interdisciplinary theological inquiry. What are the theological grounds for undertaking these inquiries? Which aspects of doctrine and tradition lend themselves to this development, and which might resist it? What attitudes and values should theologians bring to their engagement with other disciplines, and how should they understand the multiple ways of knowing that they are increasingly expected to explore?

The Shape of This Book

In this introduction, we focus on the history of interdisciplinary inquiry and the general questions that it raises for theology as a discipline. From our perspectives in ethics, theology, law, and anthropology, we ask what these developments tell us about the present state of theology and what they predict for its future. Then, at the center of the book, six scholars present studies that grow out of their own research, engaging theology and other fields of study in new

---

1. Wentzel van Huyssteen, *Alone in the World? Human Uniqueness in Science and Theology* (Grand Rapids: Eerdmans, 2006); Jeremy Waldron, *Dignity, Rank, and Rights* (Oxford: Oxford University Press, 2012); Melvin Konner, *The Evolution of Childhood: Relationships, Emotion, Mind* (Cambridge, MA: Harvard University Press, 2010).

and creative ways. At the end of the volume, a theologian returns to these questions with a constructive view of the possibilities available to theology as it faces the challenges and opportunities of this new interdisciplinary intellectual environment.

The six essays in interdisciplinary theology reflect central concerns of each author's scholarship over many years, but these studies in particular grew out of their work at the Center of Theological Inquiry during a three-year program, funded by the John Templeton Foundation, that brought teams of scholars into residence for focused, interdisciplinary study of evolution and human nature, religious experience and moral identity, and law and religious freedom. In the first essay, "Looking at Humans through the Lens of Deep History," Celia Deane-Drummond draws on new ways of thinking about the shaping of human nature to explore the interactions between agency and evolution in niche-construction, the process by which species over time not only adapt to their environment, but also create it. A more complex evolutionary understanding of how human nature took the shape it has and how it relates to other animal life makes possible a more complex account of human nature that accords with Christian tradition without denying the integrity of scientific explanations. Viewing the questions both as a biologist and as a theologian, Deane-Drummond recognizes the aesthetic element involved in mutual understanding across disciplinary boundaries. This "art" is as essential to discovery as it is difficult to capture in formalized investigative methods.

The next three essays suggest the rich conversation that is developing between psychology, theology, and historical studies as contemporary scholars seek new insights into the moral life, biblical texts, and classic works on spirituality. Michael Spezio moves from theology to the psychology of moral identity in his essay on "The Moral Life and the Structures of Rational Selves," arguing that the rich phenomenology of the moral life available in theology can be incorporated into experimental studies of moral choice and moral commitment. Where this has been done, we find a cognitive science that is more relevant to real human lives and choices and a theology that has a better understanding of the real cases of the costly love that is the conceptual center of theological ethics.

In the next essay, "In the Divine (Mental) Image," Colleen Shantz pursues the connection between psychology and religious experience from another perspective, demonstrating that an in-depth understanding of psychology can help the biblical scholar to identify cognitive structures that make biblical accounts of human experience compelling across the distances of history and culture that separate us from the text. The adaptivity and responsiveness of human cognition, both evolutionary and individual, provide ways of thinking theologically about the human relationship to God that go beyond the static image of divine perfection that often prevails in theology.

Andrea Hollingsworth's study of Nicholas of Cusa's *De visione Dei* shows how a classic text in Western spirituality anticipates modern psychological insights into cognitive transformation. Nicholas's carefully structured spiritual exercises are clearly intended to lead his readers not only to moments of illumination, but to lasting changes in the way they understand God, the world, and themselves. A neuroscientific understanding of how experience actually changes the brain may suggest the wider relevance of the fifteenth-century theologian's insights. It also reinforces Nicholas's theological realism. Theology is not just a system of ideas. It originates in experience.

Two further essays move from considerations of psychology, evolutionary biology, and human nature to the social understanding of law and religious freedom. In "Religious Persecution and Religious Freedom," John Burgess writes about the veneration in Russian Orthodoxy of hundreds of "New Martyrs" who suffered in the persecutions that followed the Revolution of 1917. A familiar language of human rights contributes to the formulation of both political and religious accounts of religious freedom, but the idea of religious freedom that emerges in the post-Soviet church puts considerable theological pressure on ordinary Western ideas of individual freedom. It also raises questions about how individual freedom of religion can be politically meaningful without an institutional structure to support it that is more enduring and independent than the law itself.

Mary Ellen O'Connell brings together disciplinary perspectives from law, theology, and aesthetics to ask what it is that makes law compelling to human persons and human societies. That question about the nature of legal authority has become more urgent as modern law relies less and less on theology and ethics, but the disciplinary isolation of legal authority provides few answers beyond the positivist explanation that law is what is declared by those who have the authority to declare it. Moving beyond these accounts, O'Connell suggests that law's power is fundamentally aesthetic. By giving an account of a sense of awe that elicits order, she builds connections between an older, theological account of law and a more constrained, modern view of legal authority. At the same time, O'Connell's essay offers a reflection on the nature of interdisciplinary inquiry that echoes Celia Deane-Drummond's suggestion that mutual understanding across disciplinary boundaries is "premised on the classical connection between goodness, beauty, and truth."[2]

These six studies do not uncritically accept the conclusions of the other disciplines they engage, nor do they expect neuroscience, psychology, law, or philosophy to resolve disputed questions of theology. Still less do they seek to establish theology as the arbiter of disagreements about human nature and social possibilities. Rather, they represent an approach to theological inquiry that echoes developments in many different disciplines that are challenging exclusive claims from within those disciplines in order to provide an integrated view of a complex reality. These new approaches in theology engage other disciplines successfully precisely because they do not

---

2. See Celia Deane-Drummond, "Looking at Humans through the Lens of Deep History," p. 15 in this volume.

seek to eliminate differences. Their work is characterized not by a single method of investigation or by a defining ideological commitment, but by habits of mind that lead to shared understanding and make further investigation possible.

Among those habits of mind, this introduction focuses especially on the virtues of humility and hope. To see why they are important for contemporary theology as it engages other disciplines, we must first understand the contrasting habits of disciplinary thinking that seem to render humility and hope irrelevant. We may start by tracing how the modern research disciplines began and how theology found its place among them.

Comprehensive Understanding and Competing Positivisms

In many early traditions of thought, the search for knowledge aimed at a comprehensive understanding of reality, binding together what the Greeks distinguished as theoretical and practical reason, or discerning the connection between cosmic order and ritual action that was central to ancient Chinese thought. In this way, the sage or the philosopher sought a principle of unity behind the multiplicity of appearances and experiences and located humanity in relation to that principle in a way that provided meaning for life and orientation for choice and action. Christian theology as it emerged out of the life of the early church understood knowledge of God in similar terms, and Augustine's interweaving of classical cosmology, biblical narrative, and religious experience set directions for the great systems of Thomas Aquinas and other medieval theologians. This aspiration is also found in Calvin and other Reformers, notwithstanding a certain early modern skepticism about metaphysics and classical learning that we encounter in nominalist philosophy and some Protestant theologians.

Skepticism, however, soon gained the upper hand, giving rise to a new kind of search for knowledge that narrowed the focus of inquiry and changed its goal. Instead of a comprehensive under-standing of reality, the philosophers—some of whom could now, in fact, be called scientists—sought certainty. In contrast to speculative generalizations about reality as a whole, certainty could be achieved by starting with the right kind of information and organizing it according to rigorous methods of investigation into a body of ev-idence that could be tested by anyone with the same specialized competence. What these investigators shared, then, was a *discipline*.

The knowledge thus secured was not comprehensive, but it was reliable, at least so far as the shared methods of a discipline could make it so. Perhaps, indeed, it was reliable because it was shared. It was not identified with one great thinker who might have rivals or critics. It was not associated with the systems of religious doc-trine that had proved so divisive during the Renaissance and the Protestant Reformation. Knowledge became the collective work of a multitude of investigators who shared the same way of working. Not limited to a particular school or geographic location, disciplines could become universal. At the same time, however, their methods set limits on what could be known. Large parts of what had previ-ously passed for knowledge would be dismissed as incomprehensi-ble or unverifiable, and things that were not subject to disciplined investigation became simply unknowable. But the method provided certainty in those matters that were open to investigation.

It is difficult to say exactly when this quest for certainty re-placed the goal of comprehensive understanding. Some associate disciplinary thinking with the rise of experimental science, which had to establish its own methods of investigation to distinguish itself from the more speculative natural philosophy that preceded it. But it took some time for reflection on these methods to harden into the claim that empirical evidence alone provides the starting point for knowledge, and experimental science was not the only model for disciplinary thinking. The possibilities became clearer in the twentieth century, by which time similar claims about the scope of knowledge were made in many fields of inquiry: Law must begin with the rules established by legal authority, with other sources excluded from a scientific view of the subject. As Mary Ellen O'Connell observes in her essay, "Law students were—and still are—taught to look at the evidence in a judicial opinion to discover the rule, much as a botanist would study a plant to learn the laws of nature."[3] Similarly, anthropology can only be scientific if it reduces cultural patterns to biology; or, alternatively, it can only be scientific if it focuses on cultural particularity and ignores biology. A political science is possible only if it reduces the sources of policy to national interest. Method could even become the criterion of meaning for language in general, with claims that cannot be verified rendered meaningless, incapable of being either true or false. Or, in a more generous view of ordinary language, meaning could be fixed by disciplined study of how a word is used, independently of complications arising from the idea that words refer to some extra-linguistic reality.

Taken together, these developments assign what can be known to various methods of investigation and raise a new question about whether it makes sense to talk about "reality" at all. Is there any place to stand outside of these various disciplinary constructs and ask what they are all talking about? It is characteristic of a discipline that it allows considerable scope for argument, disagreement, and even skepticism within the discipline, while generally insulating itself from critical or skeptical claims from outside. As this sort of disciplinary thinking developed and spread into new fields of inquiry, the search for knowledge moved, gradually and with varying degrees of conviction, into a world of competing positivisms, each of which stipulates a method of knowing and reduces the object of knowledge to what the method can know.

Theology was not a mere observer of these developments, nor did it stand by idly as others constructed a world built on verified

3. See Mary Ellen O'Connell, "Crossing the Boundaries of Law, Theology, and Aesthetics," pp. 116–17 in this volume.

facts organized into scientific theories. Theology found its own theoretical frameworks in which to conduct its arguments and insulate its key ideas from external skepticism. Theologians will be familiar with the claims: Theology has a "grammar" that determines what its discourse means and renders its language inaccessible to those who have not learned how to use it. Theology rests on a "narrative" that cannot be formulated in discursive terms that would make its claims available for general discussion. Theology "enacts" an understanding of the world, rather than arguing for it. Some of these ways of explaining how theology does its work are developed in considerable detail. Others remain little more than metaphors for ways of knowing that differ sharply from scientific methods. This emphasis on consistency in doctrine, continuity with tradition, or even what some have called a "positivism of revelation" took shape over the course of the twentieth century and gave theology a more confessional stance. The question became whether an account of God's dealing with humanity is possible unless other kinds of knowledge are excluded.

Many considerations contributed to the emergence of these ways of doing theology, which are by no means simply reactions to scientific and historical criticisms of religion. A new appreciation of biblical language and biblical worldviews plays a part, as does a morally important impulse to prevent the usurpation of theological legitimacy by new forms of political or cultural totalitarianism. Nevertheless, it is important to see that these ways of understanding theological discourse make it difficult to engage with central ideas in other disciplines on their own terms. A theological claim about human motivation is simply incommensurable with a psychological account, it might be said, while disagreements about sin and grace, justification and righteousness remain within the grammar of the doctrines and cannot be argued one way or another from the evidence of neuroscience.

The Possibilities for Interdisciplinary Inquiry

The age of disciplinary thinking achieved its full development in the middle of the twentieth century. That we are now able to see the limits of the disciplines may be an indication that we are ready to move beyond them. In recent decades, universities and research centers tightly organized along departmental and disciplinary lines have begun to open up possibilities for interdisciplinary inquiry or to set up centers and programs that bring scholars together around religion, law, human development, or other subjects that require an integrated view of the results of highly specialized research. There is, in fact, enough experience with this kind of inquiry that those who organize it have begun to publish their methods for initiating the interdisciplinary dialogues and set out the conditions that lead to successful collaborations.[4]

We might see this new interest in interdisciplinary dialogue as refocusing attention on the object of knowledge, rather than the method of investigation. Human beings, political systems, religions, planets, and poetry are complicated things. Those who want to understand them will study them from different angles, testing the results of different disciplines against one another, and recombining them for their own purposes, especially when those purposes are practical, political, or educational, rather than refinement of the disciplinary method. Perhaps, indeed, we should call these inquiries multidisciplinary, rather than interdisciplinary. They draw on a number of different disciplines—any number, in fact, that have something of interest to say—and their primary concern is not to engage them on their methodological differences, but to develop a more complete account of the social, natural, or intellectual object that is the focus of the various disciplinary investigations.

4. See, for example, Myra Strober, *Interdisciplinary Conversations: Challenging Habits of Thought* (Stanford, CA: Stanford University Press, 2010); Carolyn Brettell and James Hollifield, eds., *Migration Theory: Talking Across Disciplines* (New York: Routledge, 2014).

Agustín Fuentes and Wentzel van Huyssteen take the dialogue a step further by calling attention to the *transdisciplinary* interaction that can modify the disciplines themselves in the course of multidisciplinary investigations.[5] As researchers assimilate the results of other methods of inquiry, revise their own methods, and formulate new questions in light of what they have learned, the lines drawn when disciplines set their own boundaries begin to blur. Skepticism about other ways of knowing gives way as disciplines converge on a common object of interest or a common task. Critical attitudes are replaced by improvisation, curiosity, or even—as we will suggest in a moment—humility.

Transdisciplinarity, however, is not a new discipline, re-creating methodological rigidity on a more abstract level. We might think of it rather as a new realism, acknowledging that the things we study are not identical with the ways our disciplines construct them. This realism is practical, rather than theoretical. It warns even those investigators most committed to their own disciplines that the objects of their study may surprise them, and it suggests that if their work has a purpose beyond maintaining their reputation for methodological rigor, they need to pay special attention to the questions they would not have thought to ask.

Theological Realism

Precisely because transdisciplinary inquiry is not a new discipline, each discipline must find its own way into these discussions, explaining in its own terms what it expects to gain from them and identifying what, nevertheless, it is not prepared to give up. How, then, does theology move beyond the defense of its recently constructed disciplinary boundaries? What are the theological reasons for taking such a risky step?

5. Agustín Fuentes, "Blurring the Biological and Social in Human Becomings," in *Biosocial Becomings: Integrating Social and Biological Anthropology*, ed. Tim Ingold and Gisli Palsson (Cambridge: Cambridge University Press, 2013), 42–58.

One answer is that theology is from the beginning implicitly realist. Despite the emphasis in recent theology on narrative, doctrine, or the distinctive "grammar" of theological discourse, theology assumes that the world is in itself ordered and intelligible. This is the central idea of the account that begins the Hebrew scriptures. God gives order to the world God creates and includes in that order human beings who are able to understand it. A chaotic world that has no order except what our minds impose is a world in which there would be no God for talk about God to refer to, nor would the world be God's creation if its order remained entirely unknown or inaccessible to our minds. The world is an intelligible whole in which all things are related to one another and to God.[6]

This theological realism is not quite the same thing as scientific realism. Interdisciplinary theological inquiry does not begin in the manner of an earlier natural theology to find design in nature and make inferences to the existence and intentions of the designer. But if order and intelligibility are theological claims, rather than scientific discoveries, one task of theology will always be to account for the disorder, chaos, and incommensurability that are inevitable in our experience and part of our knowledge. The universe, as it has been said, is not only stranger than we think. It is stranger than we *can* think. A natural theology that makes order and intelligibility something we can grasp in its entirety must reject this strangeness or try to explain it away, and the natural theology that was built on the discoveries of Newton's physics eventually collapsed under the weight of this burden.

Theological realism need not reject the evidence of disorder, whether it takes the form of quantum uncertainty or the problem of evil. The assumption of intelligibility guides the search for order, but realism warns us that intelligibility does not guarantee that order

6. The idea that reality is ordered by the relation that all things have to one another and to God is developed in recent theology especially in the work of H. Richard Niebuhr and James Gustafson. See Douglas Ottati, "A Collaborative Manner of Theological Reflection," p. 137 in this volume.

will be found, or that our existing ideas and methods have found it. Nevertheless, the reason why theology can move from dialogue with evolutionary biology, to social psychology, and then to comparative law or economics, is that theology assumes that there is a connection between the order in atoms and the order of galaxies, between the order of a living organism and the order of a just society, or between the order of a fugue and the order of an ecosystem. Only God can know this order in its entirety, and many of the connections will remain, for the foreseeable future, unknown to any human inquiry. Even the most comprehensive theoretical accounts generated by different methods of investigation will be subject to revision and will leave large swathes of the world of human experience out of consideration. But the conviction that all things are related to one another in intelligible ways is not a conclusion drawn from successful efforts to render them intelligible. It begins with the theological conviction that all things are related to God. Theology has no algorithms that predict how these inquiries will turn out, but order and intelligibility suggest that different ways of knowing will commend their findings in part by their convergence with the results of other ways of knowing.

This theological realism may, however, be viewed uneasily by theologians who fear that it means that theological conclusions, too, are subject to reconsideration and revision in light of other investigations. In a secular age in which the theological account of order and intelligibility will not be taken for granted, it may seem preferable to resort to various forms of theological constructivism or idealism, in which the conclusions of theology are cast in terms that simply do not relate to other kinds of claims. Theology may simply seem unintelligible to those who do not share the theologian's starting point. How can a discourse about grace freely given connect with the economists' discourse about scarcity? The theological idealist can thus begin with an apology to the more general audience. It is not just that some things theology says will be hard to connect to your physics, psychology, or economics. The whole thing is going to be incomprehensible from the outset.

For these theologians, theological realism will seem altogether too willing to surrender theological truth to scientific criticism. The realist appears to be intellectually compromised, or perhaps just lazy and a bit too willing to borrow from other people's discoveries. Or, as we will see in a moment, the realist may appear to be guilty of a worse kind of moral weakness, yielding to mere power masquerading as moral and religious truth. But before we turn to this more serious point of contention between these different ways of understanding theology in relation to other disciplines, we must make one more attempt to say exactly what the commitment to theological realism implies about how we understand the world as a unified and intelligible whole.

Treating the results of different lines of investigation as coherent with and informative for theological conclusions does not imply that all theological claims can be reduced to other kinds of statements about the world. A theological realist may hold to the idea of a transcendent God.[7] She will want to formulate that idea in a way that is intelligible to a scientific materialist, even if the materialist concludes in the end that the idea is false. What the theological realist rejects is the claim that the question whether God transcends the world can be resolved into a question about whether the claim is meaningful in some other, nontheological way. This is not because theological claims follow their own rules or have their own grammar. It is because the world itself transcends each of the available ways of knowing it, including theological ways of knowing. Claims about the world can be meaningful from any disciplinary starting point, but all of them are necessarily incomplete. Theological realism proceeds on the assumption that the results of various investigations will converge on a coherent way of understanding

7. Not all theological realists do hold this. Various forms of theological materialism or naturalism suggest that God is best understood as immanent within or emergent from processes that can be studied by scientific methods.

the world, but it also recognizes that any given result is subject to revision and may at the limits simply have to be abandoned. That is why the realist proceeds more cautiously than an earlier kind of natural theology did when it comes to pressing the results of scientific investigation into service as theological propositions. But theological realism also refuses to turn theological propositions into limits on what we can see in the world.

Theology and Politics

These considerations become pressing in a more practical way when interdisciplinary theological inquiries extend beyond the natural and social sciences to include law, politics, and economics. To be sure, science has challenged traditional religious beliefs on many points of practice—the understanding of race and gender differences, for example, or the causes of mental illness. But there are ways of understanding social and political systems that pose such a radical challenge to any connection between theology and politics that the very idea of an interdisciplinary understanding of how these systems work becomes suspect.

This challenge often accompanies idealist or constructivist theologies that construe all human authority in relation to God's authority. In extreme form, this account of the construction—or perhaps we should say the deconstruction—of human authority renders the concept of authority apart from God unintelligible, except as a cover for some particular interest. Human authority is the contingent outcome of a struggle for power, and an accurate account of how a political community comes into being is reducible to a narrative of how power has been exercised and submission obtained. Theology often plays a role in these narratives, whether by providing sacred or charismatic authority that cannot be accounted for entirely in material terms or, in more recent forms of political theology, by providing a voluntarist account of divine sovereignty that modern forms of political sovereignty vainly attempt to emulate. Such attempts at earthly sovereignty meet with varying degrees of success, but from this theological perspective, political sovereignties are always illusory.

The contemporary theological realist must be honest about the role of power in history and vigilant against accepting any kind of social role for religion that seems simply to legitimate the existing way of doing things. But it is important, too, not to accept an oversimplified account of human personality and human community that fails to explain the actual choices that people make when confronted with the facts of political life. The reduction of political authority to questions of power often leaves us unable to make a discriminating judgment between better and worse regimes and policies. We have then only some version of the general critique of all forms of authority in which one power really cannot be distinguished from another.

By contrast, interdisciplinary theological inquiry seeks a role for a normative account of human nature in ethics and politics. Properly understood, this is not a matter of asserting a place for theology in discussions from which it has sometimes been excluded. Questions about the role and limits of religious belief in public argument will no doubt continue to be debated, but that is not the question in view here. It is rather the relevance of interdisciplinary discussion to the formation of the full account of human goods and possibilities on which real choices often depend. Contemporary theological realism does not derive propositions about God strictly from the results of other investigations. It turns to natural and social sciences, not for natural theology, but for theological anthropology, an account of human nature that is intelligible both in a theological understanding of humanity's relation to God and in biological, psychological, and sociological understandings of human flourishing. As with the descriptive investigation considered earlier, this inquiry proceeds on the assumption that the results of various normative investigations will converge on a coherent way of understanding the world, but it also recognizes that any given result is subject to revision and may have to be abandoned.

Humility and Hope

As we have already observed, there is no way of calculating in advance which of our inquiries will have to be abandoned and which will produce results. Nor is there a uniform plan that works with every pair of disciplines. As often happens with a new field of inquiry, we have an intuition about the habits of mind that make the inquiry work well before we can fully explain how to go about it. We might call these habits of mind "interdisciplinary virtues." Like the virtues that Aristotle first cataloged for us, these habits are both essential to success in the activity to which they relate and cultivated by participation in it.

The first of these habits is *humility*. Theological realism adopts a certain humility toward what it knows and toward its own limitations. The gaps in our knowledge are not easily identified, nor are the distortions in our thinking likely to become apparent first to ourselves. What we can hope for is a collaboration that offers some reason to think that we have expanded our knowledge and identified some of our errors.

In practice, humility in interdisciplinary theological inquiry means that we engage the prevailing assumptions of other disciplines as the starting point for discussion. A theology that proclaims the abundance of God's grace may nonetheless take the economists' assumption of scarcity as a starting point for discussion, and a theology that speaks of God's purposes in creation may, in search of understanding, engage a scientific materialism that traces all outcomes to prior physical causes. Of course, these other disciplines are today becoming more and more aware of their own key assumptions. Because their starting points, too, will include an account of the limits of knowledge, there may well be active controversies within economics, or biology, or legal theory about the assumptions on which the discipline rests. Theology will want to take these controversies into consideration, become well informed about them, and incorporate them into the interdisciplinary dialogue. But it will rarely be productive in these inquiries for the theologian to begin with a comprehensive theological critique of the assumptions that make another discipline possible.

It is even less likely to be helpful for the theologian to determine in advance what the political theorist, the biologist, or the psychologist needs to take on from theology, as though the theologian knows what the other discipline cannot provide for itself. As Karl Barth suggested, the question whether theology has anything to contribute to other disciplines must be answered by the disciplines themselves.[8]

Like all maxims of intellectual humility, this one is ad hoc and admits of exceptions. It is impossible for a theologian to engage in interdisciplinary inquiry, as opposed to the occasional polite conversation, with someone who denies that moral and theological propositions can be true or false. Likewise, a discipline whose premises revealed themselves upon critical examination to be racist, exploitative, or simply false would not be a good candidate for interdisciplinary theological inquiry.

The paradox of humility, of course, is that the disposition to accept the premises of another discipline for purposes of interdisciplinary inquiry rests on the realist presumption that all such premises are limited, subject to distortion, and even, in the extreme case, false. The theologian's humility should, if carried through with strict logical consistency, lead to a demand for similar humility from other disciplines in return. Interdisciplinary theological inquiry would indeed be easier if humility were more widespread and more evenly distributed across the range of potential disciplinary

8. Karl Barth, *Evangelical Theology: An Introduction* (Grand Rapids: Eerdmans, 1979), 194.

dialogue partners. But humility is not a virtue that can be cultivated in ourselves by trying to impose it on others.

What works better than trying to impose humility is engaging a second habit, namely, *hope*. Part of the way that we engage people from other disciplines is by emphasizing the moral significance of the questions we want to discuss with them. People will be willing to risk the loss of methodological rigor and even to have their basic assumptions challenged if they think it will make a difference to important issues of justice and human dignity. Regardless of their own faith or skepticism, people measure such choices by what they hope for. If the possibilities for real change are small, the importance of methodological rigor, professional reputation, or procedural correctness, rises inversely. Indeed, if things are likely to get worse no matter what you do, reasonable people are likely to conclude that these indices of intellectual rigor are their only bulwark against catastrophe. It is those who think that something can be done who bend the rule, stretch the limits, and reach out to unlikely partners. We often see this in community organization and the building of grass-roots political coalitions, but it applies more widely, including to the way that people behave in academic life. Big questions and large possibilities make people more willing to talk and ultimately to act.

Theologians, of course, have a professional interest in the virtue of hope. They not only engage hope in others. They define it and probe its limits. Their understanding of hope is part of the theological anthropology that they bring to interdisciplinary discussions. Since the beginning of modern scientific investigations, hope has often been taken to imply a progressive increase in knowledge, setting aside superstition and prejudice and steadily putting more and more of human life under the guidance of rational theories confirmed by experimental evidence. Of course, the superstitions to be set aside in this account of human progress often included traditional religious beliefs, but a strong current in modern theology also embraced this version of how hope takes form in history. Many theologians have welcomed each scientific advance from Copernicus through Newton, Darwin, and Einstein. Into the early twentieth century, especially in the English-speaking world, social progress was easily identified with the advancement of God's kingdom on earth.

By contrast, the disastrous results of applied science in the course of the twentieth century leave many theologians eager to distance themselves from the identification of hope with progress. In place of the belief in progress, these theologians offer a narrative of decline in which the catastrophes of the past hundred years are not accidents, tragedies, or simple human failures, but the inevitable result of the modern dissolution of the unity of moral, spiritual, and social ideals that once made a Christian civilization possible. Under the circumstances, the best we can hope for is a renewal of our moral and theological language comparable to the way that Christian monasticism restored the wreckage of classical civilization at the beginning of the Middle Ages. Short of that, we may take refuge as Christians have done since the Radical Reformation in a distinct community formed around our own identity, refusing responsibility for a larger society in which our witness will for the most part be incomprehensible.

This disagreement between what is called "sectarianism," "radical orthodoxy," or "political theology" on the one hand and what is on the other hand called "theological humanism," "progressive theology," or what we have here called "theological realism," runs too deep to be reduced to an argument about the interpretation of current events. While most of the questions we have discussed in this essay are questions about how to do theology, this one is itself a theological question. It is a theological argument about eschatology, about history and ultimate judgment. The intensity and pervasiveness of this dispute within contemporary theology have implications for the way we organize and conduct interdisciplinary theological inquiries.

As a practical matter, however, the engagement of theology

with other disciplines favors those who hope. We seek the kingdom of God without withholding it from those who do not look for it in the same ways that we do and without expecting to find it fully present in this place or in that. We are aware of both the theological truth that this present age is passing away and the fossil record that warns us that the end of every form of life is extinction. But we are confident, on the basis of evidence not entirely drawn from experience, that God is making all things new.

1

Looking at Humans through the Lens of Deep History

A Transdisciplinary Approach to Theology and Evolutionary Anthropology

CELIA DEANE-DRUMMOND

Why should theologians be concerned about evolutionary anthropology when coming up with a theological treatise on what it means to be human? The history that theologians are most likely to address stems from that related to the last two thousand or so years, focusing specifically on texts of the New Testament or early church history. Given the uncertainties in that more recent history, once we move back many millennia to the dawn of human emergence, "history" becomes ever more fragmented, a series of puzzles hinted at through patchy yet elusive archaeological clues that require almost an artistic sensibility for their interpretation. Some have called such a period *prehistory*, since it is before any written records, even if hints at inner mental transitions begin to show up in the form of dye markings or scratches on the surfaces of rock or bone.[1] In this essay I tackle the question of early human origins by beginning

---

1. This idea has emerged from the evolution of wisdom project led by Celia Deane-Drummond and Agustín Fuentes currently under way at the University of Notre Dame. For a good overview of published material see Kim Sterelny, *The Evolved Apprentice: How Evolution Made Humans Unique* (Cambridge, MA: MIT, 2012).

with a discussion of the biblical narrative in Genesis from two contrasting perspectives, namely, that of Roman Catholic theologian Karl Rahner and that of Jewish philosopher Alan Mittleman. Both scholars raise interesting questions about the significance of what it means to be human in light of humanity's gradual emergence. Evolutionary biologists who have considered early human history are divided as to the extent to which biological and cultural aspects of human becoming are most significant. How far and to what extent scientists might be able to engage with any theological and philosophical interpretations depends on prior epistemological commitments. Wentzel van Huyssteen has charted an interdisciplinary approach that deliberately brings theology and science together in a common transversal space. There are, however, some risks associated with his preferred methodology that I flesh out in more detail through a discussion of evolutionary anthropology using the lens of theo-drama and niche construction, both of which, I argue, are relevant to understanding the history of early human origins. I end up arguing that such analogies in a transdisciplinary mode of thinking are more like artistic appreciations or resonances, where scholars in each discipline retain their disciplinary integrity but are prepared to shift their perspectives through that exchange.

In one sense theologians are already familiar with deep history, in that the prehistory of the human race is read into the early chapters of the book of Genesis, leading to a trend within the more conservative Protestant and Roman Catholic traditions at least, to insist on a claim for the literal historicity of Adam and Eve. Coming to terms with that historicity in a way that still makes sense in an evolutionary context is a perennial challenge for serious and philosophically minded evangelical scholars.[2] At the same time, more explicitly in the Catholic tradition, any resistance to the view that there was an originating human couple, otherwise known as mono-

2. James Smith, "What Stands on the Fall? A Philosophical Exploration," in *Evolution and the Fall*, ed. William T. Cavanaugh and James K. A. Smith (Grand Rapids: Eerdmans, 2016).

genism, could threaten a belief in original sin, and so, the argument goes, would potentially threaten both human responsibility for evil and the narrative of salvation. Karl Rahner explains the logic of this position lucidly when he claims that

> original sin simply means that man, because he is a descendant of Adam, belonging to this historical, human, family, ought to possess divine grace but does not do so. Grace is conferred on him only if he is also one who has been redeemed by Jesus Christ. But both things are based on this bodily community of shared descent: the fact that according to God's plan man was to be endowed with sanctifying grace, divine life, divine nearness and divine glory; and the fact that he does not actually have all this.[3]

For that reason, Rahner devotes a whole chapter in the first volume of his major theological treatise, *Theological Investigations*, to a discussion of monogenism, concluding towards the end of this chapter that "polygenism as an object of divine action is impossible."[4] Yet talk of impossibility for God might incur some nervousness on the part of the reader, especially in view of the research emerging from evolutionary sciences. Rahner believed, of course, that he was writing at a time when the research in this aspect of human history was extremely hazy. So, for him, "since the beginning of mankind is primordial history, it lies outside the scope of natural science, it has a certain historical transcendence and cannot be examined as if it were one element among others in our history."[5] Primordial history therefore has the same kind of haziness as the distant future

---

3. Karl Rahner, *Theological Investigations,* vol. 17, *Jesus, Man and the Church,* trans. Margaret Kohl (London: Darton, Longman & Todd, 1981), 73.

4. Karl Rahner, *Theological Investigations,* vol. 1, *God, Christ, Mary and Grace,* trans. Cornelius Ernst (London: Darton, Longman & Todd, 1961), 291.

5. Karl Rahner, "Original Justice," in *Concise Oxford Dictionary of Theology,* 2nd ed., ed. Karl Rahner and Herbert Vorgrimler (London: Burns & Oates, 1983), 353–54.

expected at the end of history, and in that sense he insists that "[o]f their very nature, the reality of primordial history and eschatology is farthest removed from our idea of them."[6]

There are two aspects that are worth considering here. The first is a more general claim about whether the early chapters of Genesis really do say something significant about human origins. The second claim has to do with evolutionary anthropology, how far the prehistory that Rahner assumes really is as unknown as he implies. It is worth considering the first in more detail by examining in particular the work of a Jewish philosopher, Alan Mittleman, who has worked on the question of human origins in the light of contemporary science in a way that is highly illuminating for the broader discussion within Christian theological debates. Mittleman argues that the early part of Genesis is not intended to be a human origin story at all. Rather, the narratives are about a cultural phenomenon, how human beings fit in the natural world and their ethical responsibilities.[7] Yet, even in this qualified view there is still a clash between the naturalistic view and that of Judaism and other Abrahamic faiths, for in the biblical text human beings are always purposeful creations of God. Mittleman is correct to flag briefly the debates about the role of purpose in evolutionary theory; but it is often a functional sense of purpose, rather than an overarching or grand narrative about ultimate purposes. The language of the ultimate, if it is used at all, more often than not collapses back into forms of genetic essentialism. In the Jewish tradition humans do not just appear, as in a moment of emergence from other animals, but their appearance reflects a deliberative act of God, so "what is unmistakably clear is that God takes a moment for deliberation. He does not just command. He considers." The result is that "[t]he human being is a product of reflection and choice."[8]

6. Rahner, "Original Justice," 354.

7. Alan Mittleman, *Human Nature and Jewish Thought: Judaism's Case for Why Persons Matter* (Princeton: Princeton University Press, 2015).

8. Mittleman, *Human Nature*, 49.

But, rather than work out how such a view might cohere with evolutionary perspectives, he sees such a text as pointing to something significant about ourselves, so "[r]ecursive thought is distinctly human." Nonetheless, he is not arguing for a strong account of human exceptionalism, since "[h]uman beings are at best contingently not categorically superior to other beings."⁹ The combination of both human nobility along with humanity's pathetic or even negligible aspect provides an ambivalence that is common to human experience. He then makes the somewhat surprising claim that image also means literal physical resemblance, functioning as God's presence, in the same way that Adam passes on his likeness and image to his son, Seth. Humans become co-creators with God through propagation. But the rabbinic speculation on this text interprets the form that Adam shares with God as "energetic and radiant" rather than concrete or palpable, and it is this that is passed down the generations.¹⁰ The common ancestor assures the moral equality of all humans. After Adam's sin, looking like God is no longer possible—what remains is *acting like God*, imitating the divine, which implies the exercise of responsibility. And such responsibility includes procreation and taking responsibility for the next generation.

Mittleman includes this and other rabbinic speculation about the moral ambiguities of human nature; some even arguing that, given human propensity for evil, it might have been better if humanity had not been created. And more fascinating is the idea that the evil force or inclination is a "divinely created force" that can be overcome by study of the Torah. Human rule over the animals is therefore a God-given mandate. Cain mixed up the command and thought that humans were the same as animals, which led to the murder of his brother. Through the rabbis of the Talmud, Jewish thought parsed "all present animals as cognitively diminished

9. Mittleman, *Human Nature*, 49.
10. Mittleman, *Human Nature*, 53.

versions of human beings"[11] rather than humans as cognitively enhanced animals. Animal liability as moral agents is therefore common in the Talmud. But most importantly, the tendency to do wrong comes from our human nature, rather than hybridity with animals. The Jewish tradition thus cuts to some extent both ways; on the one hand humans are encouraged to rule the natural world, but in a manner that reflects God's rule; on the other hand the evil that they do is their own responsibility, rather than stemming from their animalistic tendencies. Mittleman carefully navigates his way through these sources by pointing to the ambiguities in the literature about human beings, especially that relating to the soul and the self, the formation of Adam as a living creature, and soul and body as both fragile and fleeting. Yet while the soul is not "trapped" in the body, there is room for a notion of a temporarily separated soul at death, whose final destiny is with a restored body. It is Jewish philosopher Joseph Albo's view on the soul that is perhaps the most interesting; that the most distinctive capacity of the human soul is not so much pure intellection, but loving service of God.[12]

The history of interpretation of the Genesis text presses beyond its particular meaning in either a Jewish or Christian context, so the question that has to be resolved is how far and to what extent such claims are justified. Does the whole pillar of Christian salvation, or even belief in the goodness of God, fall like a house of cards once Adam and Eve are no longer historical figures, the originators of human history? Is the significance of Adam and Eve often understood in Christian theology in terms of their role in instigating right moral action fully satisfying in the light of the long Jewish history of interpretation that claims much more than this? Until at least some account is taken of contemporary evolutionary anthropology, these theological puzzles remain unresolved.

11. Mittleman, *Human Nature*, 63.
12. Mittleman, *Human Nature*, 77.

Evolutionary Science and Theological Foundations

With respect to Rahner's second claim of the impossibility of reaching into this historical period with the tools of natural science, many evolutionary scientists are not averse to making strong claims about what it means to be human in the light of early hominin evolution. One key unresolved debate remains the precise relationship between human biological endowment and cultural influences in shaping the emergence of the modern human mind. Evolutionary psychologists like Steven Pinker resist the idea that the human mind is simply a blank slate, while philosophers such as Jesse Prinz challenge such seeming biological reductionism, favoring the importance of cultural and social influences.[13] Dichotomies such as these seem wooden to many evolutionary anthropologists, who prefer to put forward the idea that, in those societies that display "culture," there is a much more blurred boundary of "natureculture" that resists presupposing either of the above alternatives.[14]

Ever since Wentzel van Huyssteen presented the case for interdisciplinarity as critical for understanding the human person, the concept that there might be what he terms illuminating "*transversal spaces*" between different disciplines has been clearly on the horizon.[15] In his own words, van Huyssteen claims that

13. Jesse Prinz, *Beyond Human Nature: How Culture and Experience Shape the Human Mind* (London/New York: W. W. Norton, 2012); Steven Pinker, *The Blank Slate: The Modern Denial of Human Nature* (New York: Penguin, 2002). For further commentary, C. Deane-Drummond, "Human Natures: Moving Us Forward?" in *Verbs, Bones, and Brains: Interdisciplinary Perspectives on Human Nature*, ed. A. Fuentes and Aku Visala (Notre Dame: University of Notre Dame Press, 2016).

14. While the term was originally coined by Donna Haraway in *The Companion Species Manifesto: Dogs, People and Significant Others* (Chicago: Prickly Paradigm, 2003), it has been taken up and used by an increasing number of anthropologists, including Agustín Fuentes; it has been influential in my own work, completed at CTI, *The Wisdom of the Liminal* (Grand Rapids: Eerdmans, 2014).

15. Wentzel van Huyssteen, *Alone in the World? Human Uniqueness in Science and Theology* (Grand Rapids: Eerdmans, 2009), 20.

transversal reasoning does not imply that scientific data, paradigms, or worldviews, can be transported into theology to there set the agenda for theological reasoning. Transversal reasoning does mean that theology and science can share concerns and converge on commonly identified conceptual problems such as the problem of human uniqueness. These mutually critical tasks presuppose, however, the richness of the transversal moment in which theology and evolutionary anthropology may indeed find amazing connections and overlapping intersections on issues of human origins and uniqueness.[16]

His view resists *foundationalism* of all kinds in the interest of open discussion between scientists and theologians, where at least some common ground can be established. By foundationalism he means "the thesis that all our beliefs can be justified by appealing to some item of knowledge that is self-evident or indubitable. Foundationalism in this epistemological sense therefore always implies the holding of a position inflexibly and infallibly, because in the process of justifying our knowledge-claims, we are able to invoke ultimate foundations on which we construct the evidential support systems of our various convictional beliefs."[17] While this perspective is often rejected in favor of a relativistic nonfoundationalism, van Huyssteen presses for what he terms a *post*foundationalist view, analogous to the rise of postmodern discourse.[18] The diffi-

16. Van Huyssteen, "Human Origins and the Emergence of a Distinctively Human Imagination: Theology and the Archeology of Personhood," in *Verbs, Bones, and Brains.*

17. Wentzel van Huyssteen, *Essays in Postfoundationalist Theology* (Grand Rapids: Eerdmans, 1999), 2–3.

18. Postfoundationalism means, for van Huyssteen, first, an acknowledgment of context, and the way knowledge is interpreted in the light of experience. Second, it means a way of "pointing creatively" beyond a particular local community, group, or culture towards a "plausible form of inter-disciplinary conversation." Van Huyssteen, *Essays*, 4. Of course, two problems with this particular approach spring to mind. The first is that science itself is, to some extent, still embedded in culture, and secondly the idea that any group or culture could somehow be supervened in

culty, of course, is how to arrive at what he calls "responsible critical judgment" in making epistemological decisions that he believes are common for theology and the secular sciences,[19] while at the same time avoiding a narrow "fideism" that accepts the teachings of the church without question.

Is Rahner a foundationalist in the sense that van Huyssteen defines this term? In one sense he is, insofar as he adheres to the established magisterium, even if he interprets that teaching in a new way. But more conservative scholars would find even Rahner moving too far away from that teaching. It is also important to note that a scholar such as Pierre Teilhard de Chardin, who dealt with this early period of history in his work *The Human Phenomenon*, was silenced by the church in his lifetime.[20] Since then there has been a gradual accommodation of some of his ideas by the magisterium, though the most favored ideas relate to the cosmic status of the mass, rather than to his explicit evolutionary theism.[21] Teilhard, in my view, was

---

the way he suggests is desirable is likely to be unrealistic. My own view is therefore rather less syncretic compared with that of van Huyssteen, simply because I believe that, in spite of qualifications regarding theology's hermeneutical task, in the end theology offers its own distinctive metaphysics that cannot be accommodated so readily to that of scientific epistemology.

19. Van Huyssteen, *Essays*, 23.

20. Pierre Teilhard de Chardin, *The Human Phenomenon* (New York: Harper, 1959). This book was published posthumously.

21. It is noteworthy that the cosmic status of Christ and the significance of the mass are referred to by Pope Francis. He refers to Teilhard discreetly by his suggestion that "[t]he ultimate destiny of the universe is in the fullness of God, which has already been attained by the risen Christ, the measure of the maturity of all things (§83)," with a footnote that claims, "against this horizon we can set the contribution of Fr Teilhard de Chardin." Towards the end of his encyclical he refers to the Eucharist as "the living center of the universe, the overflowing core of love and of inexhaustible life (§236)." Such a view is very much in the spirit of Teilhard's thought, and it is significant that both his papal predecessors also welcomed Teilhard's elevation of the status of the Eucharist. For example, Pope Benedict XVI explicitly affirmed Teilhard's "great vision" of the cosmic liturgy in his homily on 24 July 2009, where he celebrated vespers with the faithful of Aosta. http://w2.vatican.va/content/benedict-xvi/en/homilies/2009/documents/hf_ben-xvi_hom_20090724_vespri-aosta.html, accessed August 6, 2015. The idea of a cos-

still far too wedded to a synthetic approach to Christology and evolution for him to be widely appropriated in the way that some of his
supporters imply, but his views on the cosmic Eucharist are rather
more palatable.[22] Evolutionary history is also moving and changing,
opening a ready trap for the unaware. Jack Mahoney, for example,
puts forward a thesis that claims that doctrines such as original sin,
the fall, and so on are no longer viable in the light of contemporary
evolutionary science, a science that, according to him, is marked by
a form of genetic determinism and strong neo-Darwinianism.[23] Yet
he is still prepared to hold onto a belief in Christ as both human and
divine, and belief in the resurrection, claiming not just that Christ
is savior of the human race, but the whole world. His discussion of
evolutionary biology is somewhat outdated in the light of current
debates, and this impacts on at least some of his conclusions.

Pope Francis, whose background is in chemistry, takes Pope
John Paul II's position on evolutionary theory, by affirming evolution as a story about natural origins, but then insisting that there
is something distinct, new, with the appearance of human beings.
On the one hand, Pope Francis is ready to sign up to evolutionary
accounts inasmuch as he believes that they tell us something about
the way God created the world, and are therefore compatible with
the book of Genesis. He wants to get away from any sense that God
intervenes as if by magic in creating the natural world. Rather, his
claim that God uses the tools of evolutionary biology puts him in
line with the tradition of evolutionary theism. So, "[w]hen we read
the account of Creation in Genesis we risk imagining that God was
a magician, complete with an all powerful magic wand. But that

mic liturgy reaches back to early Orthodox theologians, who also influenced the
writing of Teilhard.

22. For further discussion, see C. Deane-Drummond, *Christ and Evolution:
Wonder and Wisdom* (Minneapolis: Fortress, 2009).

23. Jack Mahoney, *Christianity in Evolution: An Exploration* (Minneapolis:
Fortress Press, 2011). For further discussion see Celia Deane-Drummond, "In Adam
All Die? Questions at the Boundary of Niche Construction, Community Evolution
and Original Sin," in *Evolution and the Fall*.

was not so. He created beings and he let them develop according to the internal laws with which He endowed each one, that they might develop, and reach their fullness. . . . God is not a demiurge or a magician, but the Creator who gives life to all beings."[24]

But, when it comes to a closer consideration of human beings, Pope Francis resists dissolving the uniqueness of humanity in an evolutionary account. So, on the other hand, his encyclical *Laudato Si'* claims that "[o]ur capacity to reason, to develop arguments, to be inventive, to interpret reality and to create art, along with other not yet discovered capacities, are signs of a uniqueness which transcends the spheres of physics and biology. The sheer novelty involved in the emergence of a personal being within a material universe presupposes a direct action of God and a particular call to life and to relationship on the part of a 'Thou' who addresses himself to another 'thou.' The biblical accounts of creation invite us to see each human being as a subject who can never be reduced to the status of an object."[25]

Disciplinary Integrity and the Art of Dialogue

The critical theoretical question then, arising from such a discussion, becomes how far to go in a postfoundationalist era. For Jewish scholars like Mittleman and for Pope Francis, the question of human distinctiveness leads them to resist any easy reading in light of evolutionary history. At the same time, evolutionary anthropologists are also prepared to admit distinctiveness, but would be

24. Pope Francis, Plenary Session of the Pontifical Academy of Sciences, "Address of His Holiness Pope Francis" on the Occasion of the Inauguration of the Bust in Honour of Pope Benedict XVI," Casina of Pius IV, Monday, 27 October 2014, http://w2.Vatican.Va/Content/Francesco/En/Speeches/2014/October/Documents/Papa-Francesco_20141027_Plenaria-Accademia-Scienze.html, accessed May 22, 2015.

25. Pope Francis, *Laudato Si': On Care for Our Common Home* (New York: Catholic Bishops), §81.

reluctant to register this through presupposing some direct action of God in the way that these religious traditions assert. And, in this respect, this raises a general theoretical point, namely, are there some key concepts worth retaining without which theology loses its edge as theology? For Mahoney, original sin and early human origins are an optional extra, but not belief in the redeeming power of Christ. Rahner parses out the line rather differently, and retreats into a position that allows him to claim to be adhering to the tradition, while also exploring science. But that position only works when there are gaps in the scientific knowledge. Pope Francis will accommodate science, but only so far.

Continental philosophy, insofar as it is postmodern *and* posthuman, aligns with the kind of transversal approach pioneered by van Huyssteen, but difficult decisions still have to be made about potential limits to deconstruction; about what the risks as well as the potential might be in the transversal space opened up by serious conversation between evolutionary scientists and theologians who have, at least according to their own lights, very different metaphysical and theoretical starting points.

Those who are both practicing evolutionary biologists and adherents to Christian faith with some knowledge of theology are few and far between,[26] and, I suspect, are frequently challenged to undergo a kind of internal mental gymnastics, looking at the problem through one lens and then through another. In the light of such confusion many turn to analytical philosophy to help clarify the assumptions and the logical bases behind both theological claims and scientific ones. Analytical philosophy is also helpful in cleaning up some of the weeds that can prevent adequate understanding, but, es-

---

26. Jeffrey Schloss is one such exceptional scholar, who is both practicing as a biologist and has knowledge of theology, and while he would not claim to be a theologian, does write in a way that shows intelligent engagement with this literature. See, for example, *The Believing Primate: Scientific, Philosophical, and Theological Reflections on the Origin of Religion*, ed. Jeffrey Schloss and Michael Murray (Oxford: Oxford University Press, 2009).

pecially where done in detachment from practice, it can seem just as far from lived scientific experience as from lived Christian practices. So, is it really enough just to use analytical philosophy to adjudicate the logical coherence of a scientific theory or theological statement? Continental philosophy can also commit the same error; Jacques Derrida's work on humanity's relationship with other animals, for example, was a fascinating exploration of human distinctiveness as challenged by the subjectivity of another animal, spurred on by his encounter with a cat, but still just as much removed from the knowledge arising from serious scientific study of cats in particular and other animals in general.[27] Somehow theologians need to use philosophical analyses as well as scientific theories, wisely and with rigor. Religious and theological arguments cannot be reduced to philosophy without remainder, any more than they can be reduced to science.

One original methodological approach that builds on the work of van Huyssteen is the use of Paul Ricoeur's work as a way of developing the transversal space.[28] Drawing heavily on Ricoeur's interdisciplinary theory, Ken Reynhout argues that the scientific way of approaching the world through *explanation* needs to work in dialectical relationship with theology's *search for understanding*. Ricoeur's interdisciplinary work focused on philosophy; Reynhout creatively extends his hermeneutical method to the dialogue between theology and the natural sciences, while insisting that theology not lose its bearings in tradition. Reynhout is correct to observe that there has been relatively little influence of continental philosophy on the science and religion debate. Theology can still remain faithful to itself and borrow heavily from the sciences through a sophisticated process of hermeneutics, that is, interpretation. This is not simple window dressing, but an honest attending to the specific and le-

27. Jacques Derrida, *The Animal That Therefore I Am*, ed. Marie-Louise Mallet, trans. David Wills (New York: Fordham University Press, 2008).

28. Kenneth A. Reynhout, *Interdisciplinary Interpretation: Paul Ricoeur and the Hermeneutics of Theology and Science* (Lanham, MD: Lexington Books, 2014).

gitimate challenges of the natural sciences. Ricoeur believed that understanding came through explanation; hence, the deepest theological insights come through coming to terms with the insights of the sciences. If van Huyssteen works with a postfoundational epistemology in order to arrive at a new kind of hermeneutics, Reynhout puts the order in reverse, arguing through the lens of Ricoeur for the primacy of hermeneutics for both theology and science in a way that leads to a renewed form of knowledge.

During the CTI Inquiry on Evolution and Human Nature, we encountered problems associated with the above in particular ways. Those deeply immersed in philosophical works found it hard to relate to evolutionary scientists who had particular questions in mind that pressed for resolution. Philosophers are often less anxious about finding solutions to particular scientific questions as opening up new questions arising from the enigma of human existence. The theologians among us, on the other hand, had particular concerns about how specific theological beliefs and key doctrines could become meaningful in an evolutionary context. The questions that constructive theology sought to develop were outside the radar of evolutionary biology. But we found, as we persisted in this conversation, that insights from evolutionary biology raised new and interesting questions for theology and vice versa. This method required a patience and intellectual generosity that presupposes those entering it will have a sense of ignorance of the field of the other in dialogue, but at the same time, a willingness and an openness to learn. Reynhout puts it well when he claims that "sometimes we find ourselves talking about what we assume is the same thing only to discover we are talking past one another because we actually mean different things."[29]

Hence, this opens up a new kind of methodological approach that is the true *art* of what I prefer to call transdisciplinarity; by which I mean paying close attention to the other discipline(s) in a

29. Reynhout, *Interdisciplinary Interpretation*, 153.

way that has a substantial and mutual impact, but at the same time retaining a clear sense of disciplinary integrity.[30] What that integrity might mean is, of course, contested, but each of us operates within what could be termed a "comfort zone," and the challenge is how far to move away from that while respecting limits. That is why I prefer to call this process an art; there is an aesthetic judgment here that is much harder to delineate compared with setting specific rules for conduct, and will depend on the dynamics of the particular group in question. Not all those present need to think the same way. In fact a measure of diversity encourages mental agility. My suspicion is also that this process works best when those who begin this encounter are relatively new to the experience, since those who have worked in the area of theology and science dialogue for many years might have arrived at a settled position on the "field" that itself has morphed into a new discipline. That is less engaging than witnessing the emergence of a new kind of dynamic among those who would not, habitually speaking at least, have come into contact with one another. For example, in our group, at the start of the year, some of the scientists present did not really know what theology meant and had never encountered theologians. And the term *art* is relevant in another sense, in that what emerges in mutual understanding is something that is rather closer to the truth as a result of the encounter, premised on the classical connection between goodness, beauty, and truth. Those taking part in this process are therefore not just changed in the way they think, but also, to some extent at least, changed inwardly as well.

30. Agustín Fuentes develops this idea further from the perspective of evolutionary anthropology in his article "Evolutionary Perspectives and Transdisciplinary Intersections: A Roadmap to Generative Areas of Overlap in Discussing Human Nature," *Theology and Science* 11, no. 2 (2013): 106–29.

A Constructive Alternative

This is learning, then, at its most fruitful, but such an art is not often encountered either in university education or in academic experience. In this sense I believe that the kind of theological exploration that was possible in projects such as that generated in the year when I was at CTI offers a different kind of model for undergraduate and graduate education, one that insists on the extent and degree of learning possible through genuine transdisciplinary exchange. Further, it is through questions arising from evolutionary biology in particular that growth is feasible, especially in a North American context, where the exchange is set in a context of prior suspicion and hostility. Hence, while the public image of theology and evolutionary science is colored by dyed-in-the-wool creationists or strict Darwinians whose narrow sense of scientific positivism aligns with atheism, a very different kind of approach is possible, in the public sphere as well as in specific educational contexts.

For too long theologians have been passive partners in dialogue with evolutionary science, fending off atheistic objections to religious belief through retreat or even outright hostility, or simply accommodating scientific insights without questioning them through evolutionary theism. Van Huyssteen avoids such mistakes, but then he has in effect opened up a further set of questions about the place and role of more constructive approaches to theology.

One option, taken by Sarah Coakley in her Gifford lectures, is to listen carefully to mathematically orientated evolutionary biologists like Martin Nowak[31] and develop a case for a new kind of natural theology, keeping the more explicit theological aspects as far as possible in the background.[32] Of course, as an apologetic tactic in reaching

31. Sarah Coakley's Gifford Lectures, "Sacrifice Regained: Evolution, Cooperation and God," http://www.giffordlectures.org/lectures/sacrifice-regained-evolution-cooperation-and-god (accessed November 7, 2016).

32. This is Coakley's clear intention, but the language of sacrifice conjures up

those who would not otherwise listen to theologians, this may well be successful. The status of mathematics in biology has always been high, and perhaps is particularly high even in those fields where rigorous analysis of evolutionary evidence is difficult. But, as in evolutionary psychology more generally, we should not deceive ourselves that the evidence is more substantial than it really is. As Jeff Schloss has pointed out, "The Darwinian insight can be phrased simply as: The composition of a population will change in the direction of those entities that make more copies of themselves than others. But this could not possibly be false."[33] It seems, then, that a logical truth is being co-opted as a biological law, leading to considerable doubts about the validity of naming evolution by natural selection a law at all! The problem, then, seems to be one of misplaced confidence among some evolutionary biologists. Without due care, theologians will then be at a loss as to what explicitly they might be able to contribute.

An alternative approach that I suggest is much more common among evolutionary anthropologists is that of admission of a high degree of evolutionary complexity, while refusing to give up on the search for knowledge. In such circumstances, while not necessarily sharing any specific religious belief, anthropologists can begin to ask the kinds of questions that have troubled theologians for centuries. And one such question is what are the origins of human wisdom, understood as transcendental and as transactional—perhaps even appearing in distinct hominin populations prior to the emergence of *Homo sapiens sapiens*?[34] And once sci-

---

far more visceral religious images that seem to point in a rather different direction. The final book emerging from the lectures may well clarify this point.

33. Jeffrey Schloss, "Laws of Life," in *Concepts of Law in the Sciences, Legal Studies, and Theology*, ed. Michael Welker and Gregor Etzelmüller, Religion in Philosophy and Theology 72 (Tübingen: Mohr Siebeck, 2013), 65; also in C. Deane-Drummond, "Natural Law Revisited: Wild Justice and Human Obligations to Other Animals," *Journal of the Society of Christian Ethics* 35, no. 2 (2015): 159–73.

34. The Templeton-funded *Human Distinctiveness Project*, led by Celia Deane-Drummond and Agustín Fuentes, is designed in its research element to address this question.

entists ask *these* kinds of questions, the view that evolutionary science is merely a back door to a specific type of amorality no longer applies.

A useful philosophical tool in such scenarios is that of *analogy of being*; so that just as my thoughts about the economy of God will only ever be analogies drawn from my experience of human society, so theological insight will only ever be analogies of what might be discussed in evolutionary anthropology. But God cannot be reduced to human society, nor can theology be reduced to evolution or anthropology, even if evolutionary psychologists would like to cast religion as, for example, a form of projection or displaced sensitivity to agency.[35] Once the two are fused together, problems result based on a respective jarring of two very different metaphysical presuppositions. Analogy attempts to avoid this problem by seeking what Markus Muehling has termed *resonances* at a transdisciplinary level.[36]

One resonance that I have argued for in my own work developed at CTI is the alignment of niche construction with theo-drama. Both are theoretical concepts that make claims about how human or other creaturely agency is important in shaping their respective futures. Niche construction represents a philosophical shift in the way evolutionary processes work, so evolutionary questions come under the umbrella of Niche Construction Theory (NCT), rather than simply adding it on to previous models.[37] It is particularly

35. Evolutionary psychology has tended to prefer the idea of God as an evolutionary offshoot of displaced hyperactive agency detection device (HAAD), including Christian scholars such as Justin Barrett. See J. Barrett, "Exploring the Natural Foundations of Religion," *Trends in Cognitive Science* 4, no. 1 (2000): 29–34.

36. M. Muehling, *Resonances: Neurobiology, Evolution and Theology. Evolutionary Niche Construction, the Ecological Brain and Relational Narrative Theology* (RThN 29) (Göttingen/Bristol, CT: Vandenhoeck & Ruprecht, 2014).

37. Jeremy Kendal, Jamshid J. Tehrani, and F. John Odling-Smee, "Human Niche Construction in Interdisciplinary Focus," *Philosophical Transactions of the Royal Society B* 366 (2011): 785–92. The mathematical expression of NCT is straightforward. Standard evolutionary theory assumes that an organism's state is a function of the organism and the environment ($dO/dt= f(O,E)$) and changes in the environ-

interesting in my view as it provides a significant bridge between the biological sciences and the human, cultural sciences. Standard evolution theory is "externalist" inasmuch as the environment is viewed as an "external" factor acting in order to select those internal properties that are most adapted to that environment. Natural selection in this view is the "ultimate" category that explains phenotype, including behavioral differences, and devalues "proximate" causes. Hence, standard evolution theory can include niche construction, but the "ultimate" explanation is still one rooted in natural selection. In NCT the idea of "causation" becomes problematized. So the "dichotomous proximate and ultimate distinction" is replaced by "reciprocal causation."[38] In this way niche construction works with natural selection in the evolutionary process in a dynamic interchange. Niches are themselves part of the inheritance process, so that an *interactionist* theory replaces an *externalist* theory. Niche construction emphasizes not just genetic and cultural inheritance, but also ecological inheritance as well, in dynamic interaction with the first two.[39] But envisioning cultural aspects as separate from ecological inheritance seems too constraining. Ecological and cultural inheritance under a broader "ecological" category carries the advantage of perceiving a developmental context where the physical niche is not separated from the social niche.[40]

---

ment are simply a function of that environment ($dE/dt=g(E)$). NCT, on the other hand, allows for the organism to be able to change the environment, and so can be expressed mathematically as $dO/dt=f(O,E)$ and $dE/dt=g(O,E)$.

38. Kendal et al., "Human Niche Construction," 786.

39. This threefold model of Laland et al. compares with the four dimensions of evolution suggested by Jablonka and Lamb. The difference in this case is a greater emphasis on the ecological aspects; the latter allow for niche construction, but place this in the context of behavioral change and symbolic change as two of the four dimensions of evolution. Kevin N. Laland, F. John Odling-Smee, and Marc W. Feldman, "Cultural Niche Construction and Human Evolution," *Behavioral Brain Sciences* 23 (2000): 131-75.

40. F. John Odling-Smee, "Niche Inheritance," in *Evolution: The Extended Synthesis*, ed. Massimo Pigliucci and Gerd B. Muller (Cambridge, MA: MIT, 2010), 175-207.

Theo-drama became well known in theological circles through the work of Roman Catholic theologian Hans Urs von Balthasar, who dedicated five volumes to this topic.[41] The basic concept of *theo-drama* is that the storied history of God's relationship with humanity, expressed most explicitly in the narrative of Jesus Christ, becomes more vivid and immediate when parsed out through the language of *drama*, rather than *narrative*.[42] The differences between drama and narrative are subtle but obvious once narrative is viewed as a grand narrative or *epic* that has a tendency to lose its ground of contact with a more immediate historical context. In Christology this difference is expressed as a tension between the cosmological and historical Christ, the former speaking of the principled relationship between Christ as Logos and the cosmos, while the latter refers to the life, death, and resurrection of Jesus of Nazareth.

In anthropology such differences relate to different theological anthropologies and theologies of history; so, in Ben Quash's words, "synchronic" readings of history "fail to give due attention to particulars, to the individuals, the exceptions to rules, the resistances to explanation and the densities of meaning that ask for recognition in a good description of historical reality."[43] Now, if evolutionary biology is brought into conversation with this approach, we might query how far its readings are necessarily synchronic, given strong evolutionary principles such as natural selection. A more dramatic and richly diachronic historical reading of evolution will focus on particular periods in that history.

Von Balthasar restricted his account of theo-drama to the hu-

41. See, for example, his second volume, Hans Urs von Balthasar, *Theodrama II, Dramatis Personae: Man in God*, trans. Graham Harrison (San Francisco: Ignatius Press, 1990).

42. As I have discussed in a number of volumes, including, for example, Celia Deane-Drummond, *Christ and Evolution: Wonder and Wisdom* (Minneapolis: Fortress, 2009); *The Wisdom of the Liminal: Evolution and Other Animals in Human Becoming* (Grand Rapids: Eerdmans, 2014).

43. Ben Quash, *Theology and the Drama of History* (Cambridge: Cambridge University Press, 2005), 7.

man sphere and considered evolutionary biology to be too caught up in a materialist metaphysics to be useful theologically. My own position is somewhat different. I agree that theo-drama deliberately includes God and the revelation of God in human history, including an interpretation of that history in the light of future hope, or eschatology, in a way that marks out clear metaphysical differences from secular approaches to evolutionary anthropology. So for theo-drama the overarching drama is under the providence of God, while evolutionary anthropology would deny any divine influence: at best it amounts to restraint or convergence.[44] However, that does not mean that evolutionary accounts are redundant in theological terms, since there are ways of reading evolutionary biology that are at least less hostile to those differences by speaking of *analogies* between what can be found in evolutionary terms and what is articulated through theological anthropology. I therefore press for a less exclusive and more expansive notion of theo-drama that includes other creaturely kinds in that drama, while at the same time recognizing the distinctive role of humankind, capable of a degree of freedom, will, and responsiveness to the divine intent that is not feasible for other creaturely kinds. Hence, another useful point of contact is that of *interspecies*, i.e., teasing out the special significance of human/animal relations. Here the language used by theologians and anthropology is the same, but theologians will speak about creatures and Creator, thus highlighting the significance of shared creaturely becoming.

All such discussions are of critical importance not just in terms of how we might reflect on human origins or purpose, but also on the way ethics and morality are understood. Indeed the evolution of morality is one of the hottest topics in evolutionary biology and is likely to engender equally strident reactions by theologians wishing to preserve a sense of divine agency in the world. Yet there need

---

44. Simon Conway Morris, *Life's Solution: Inevitable Humans in a Lonely Universe* (Cambridge: Cambridge University Press, 2006).

to be spaces and places where theologians, philosophers, evolutionary biologists, and anthropologists can come together in a way that leads to mutual respect, even if full consonance is less likely. Indeed, our work together at CTI made me more aware than ever of the need for careful listening, but also a resistance to too-ready consonance in the interests of peacemaking. While finding common ground is at one level exhilarating as it moves the conversation forward in a fruitful way, some dissonance is, I suggest, as necessary as the sand in the oyster shell if we, as scholars, are to produce that sought-after pearl of great price.

2

The Moral Life and the Structures of Rational Selves

Theology and Science on *Habitus*, *Imitatio*, and the
Valuation of Self and Other

MICHAEL SPEZIO

Interdisciplinarity as concept and practice invites diverse interpretations and applications among scholars working in the early
twenty-first century. Many seeking an interdisciplinary reach beyond their own discipline nevertheless restrict their practice to interpreting, deconstructing, and diminishing other disciplines with
the views they hold to be victorious and the narratives they say
hold sway. As evidenced in the introductory essay, the work of this
volume is far from such a restrictive notion of interdisciplinarity.
Instead, there is an openness to wonder and to deep engagement, a
rigorous hearing out of disciplinary approaches while at the same
time resisting the urge to "uncritically accept the conclusions of the
. . . disciplines" so engaged. There can be no expectation that "neu-

I am grateful for helpful conversations with Warren Brown, Jan Gläscher, Stanley
Hauerwas, Andrea Hollingsworth, Fr. Thomas Keating, Christian Keysers, Robin
Lovin, Kristen Renwick Monroe, Nancey Murphy, Sheryl Overmyer, Gregory Pe-
terson, Stephen Pope, Steven Quartz, Kevin Reimer, and Linda Zagzebski; and for
funding from the Science and Transcendence Advanced Research Series of the Cen-
ter of Theology and the Natural Sciences, from the Center of Theological Inquiry in
Princeton, NJ, from the John Templeton Foundation (Grant 21338), and from the
Self, Motivation, and Virtue Project (University of Oklahoma).

roscience, psychology, law, or philosophy [may] resolve disputed questions of theology."[1]

The present essay is presented in this open spirit and advocates a return to the phenomena of exemplary moral life as a way forward for new approaches in moral theology, specifically via explorations of *imitatio* and *habitus*. Such a return would be an attempt at close listening, at attention with and within the real world, practical phenomena of the morally upbuilding life, resisting the desire to allow any given theoretical perspective to overshadow a commitment to realism within both theology and science. These phenomena of the real world are, to a great extent, already recognized by a number of contemporary lines of theological inquiry into the moral life, all of which point beyond textual evidence and literary critical approaches, and in various ways draw on the examples of living communities of dedicated moral commitment and moral resistance, along with the teachers lifted up and celebrated in those communities. Ethnographic, embodied, and other contextually sensitive theologies are already expert in such close listening to community experience and example. Approaches within virtue science, or the science of moral cognition and action, would benefit greatly from careful consideration of the scholarly work being done in these theological lines, and from partnerships with the communities already highlighted in their works.

The primary intellectual challenge for virtue science is not conflict between theology and science, since such conflict is almost always the result of unspoken biases against either theology or science, and these biases are generally grounded in a lack of real understanding. Rather, the overwhelming challenge to efforts at furthering theological and scientific progress in the study of virtue is a reliance on theory and method not suitably realistic, humble, or hopeful. One sees this challenge in suboptimal and misleading

---

1. See Lovin et al., "Introduction: Theology as Interdisciplinary Inquiry," in this volume, p. xvii.

models of human nature that project unrealistic concepts of the moral self and its character. Similarly, there is a problem with experimental designs that marginalize the role of attending to moral phenomena as stable, reasoned commitments and relationships in the real lives of those in communities of stable, reasoned, moral exemplarity.

Instead of these substandard approaches, it is better to prioritize a mindfulness regarding the phenomena of interest when scholars seek to better understand together the moral self and its virtues. In adopting this approach, this paper is following the example of many traditions of moral community, as well as best practice in the scientific study of the mind, which can be seen in the example of the late Francisco Varela and his colleagues. In his seminal work reorienting the scientific study of consciousness, Varela stressed how important it is to work with those who are exemplary in their development of stable, richly conscious states.[2] Varela's emphasis may be taken to stem primarily from his scientific commitment to developing a rich and full understanding of a set of phenomena prior to, or at least in partnership with, developing robust scientific theories to address the phenomena of interest.

Varela's scientific commitment is an intellectual virtue that is reflected by the theological orientations across the essays of this volume and summarized in the opening essay. Theology is committed to a rich, descriptive account of the phenomena of life as communicated in and through symbols that point to primal meaning and formation of community and of persons. Whether those symbols are language, physical objects, music, ritual, contemplative practices, etc., theology as a discipline concerns itself with phenomenally rich expressions as it seeks to explore and give shape to the array of life-giving meanings at the core of life experiences/events.

2. Evan Thompson and Francisco J. Varela, "Radical Embodiment: Neural Dynamics and Consciousness," *Trends in Cognitive Sciences* 5 (2001): 418–25; Francisco J. Varela, "Patterns of Life: Intertwining Identity and Cognition," *Brain and Cognition* 34 (1997): 72–87.

One discerns a first movement that unites theology and science—at least in science following Varela's example—precisely in the careful engagement with the phenomena that so capture the attention of the scholar and her community. Theology need not go to science with hat-in-hand, so to speak, if this means an abject posture that looks primarily to science for meaningful accounts of phenomenal life. Similarly, scientific theories that marginalize richly meaningful phenomena in the service of more parsimonious, more beautifully intuitive models, need not be granted superior standing based primarily on that beautiful parsimony, a false simplicity. Science, especially when it omits significant life experience in the service of theoretical coherence and mechanistic beauty, needs theology to remind it of just what it seeks to understand.

Scientific and Theological Focus
on the Phenomena of Interest

Scientific approaches to the moral life, then, require theological accounts of the moral selves and communities—exemplars—that continue to inspire, those who show and invite careful engagement with ways of being human that often seem, due to a distorted and erroneous moral perception, to be quite beyond the capability of human beings. These persons and communities are both the central phenomena of interest and the means of organizing formational activity in the development of the moral life. The formational activity requires both a core around which formation can occur—the *imitatio* of exemplars and/or exemplary communities—and attention to the qualities that are so formed, conceptualized as *habitus*.

Another way of thinking about maintaining a focus on exemplars and/or exemplary communities in inquiries into the moral self comes from the perspective of ethology. Ethology is a science that prioritizes behaviors of interest by identifying them in the environments in which they emerged and for which they are well adapted for flourishing. One might think of the difference in insight gained from studying the behavior of whales in the wild versus studying the behavior of whales birthed and raised and trained to perform certain tricks for rewards in small tanks in captivity. Exemplary moral communities in the real world—whether historical or contemporary—may be thought of as places of special interest and inquiry where moral theology and virtue science meet, because of their import, sensitivity, and ability to navigate the depths of moral life in the real world with all of its complexity and resistance to easy systematization.

Consider for a moment the superficial insights into the nature of the moral life and moral mind that are gained from studying morally salient behaviors of unknown, randomly selected individuals in the laboratory, whose stable moral commitments are completely unknown. This superficial approach—by far the most commonly adopted in the cognitive science of moral action—is known as cognitive averaging. Cognitive averaging is a critically important design choice that almost never receives explicit justification in any scientific papers on moral cognition and action. Indeed, cognitive averaging is a procedure that most cognitive scientists in, say, fields of memory or attention or face processing or emotion would not support.[3] Cognitive averaging is the methodological practice of providing little or no screening, or at best minimal screening, of potential participants' abilities in a given type of cognition prior to including them in a scientific study of that cognition. Generally, cognitive scientists who study attention, perception, memory, language, emotion, etc., use screening procedures to test whether the participants in their studies of these processes understand the normative elements of the experimental tasks and stably choose according to those normative elements, even when the goal is to

3. Gregory Peterson, James Van Slyke, Michael L. Spezio, Kevin Reimer, and Warren S. Brown, "The Rationality of Ultimate Concern: Moral Exemplars, Theological Ethics, and the Science of Moral Cognition," *Theology and Science* 8 (2010): 139–61.

identify possible deficits in the processes under investigation. In cognitive studies of face processing, for example, a commonly used screening tool is the Benton Facial Recognition Task,[4] which assesses the ability to recognize faces of different people and of the same person from different angles. One can readily see, for example, that to study the mental processing involved in Spanish fluency requires working with participants who are not only fluent in Spanish but who have Spanish as their first language (their L1), complete with the cultural context and sensitivities and long-term relations that linguistic capacity entails. A fluent Spanish speaker who learned Spanish as a second language is demonstrably different—behaviorally and neurally—than one who knew only Spanish or who first discovered Spanish as an infant, in the voice of the loving caretaker, and who literally lived in and via Spanish into adulthood. If it is clear that the cognitive scientific approach to understanding Spanish, or English, or Russian, or any language must first look to L1 speakers, then the same requirement for embedded, long-term expertise is clear for any study of mathematics, of problem-solving expertise (e.g., playing chess, choreography), of logical inference, indeed for any area of cognition that includes recognized norms applied to task outcomes.

Yet most social psychological and neuroscientific studies of moral cognition and action, by way of contrast, completely ignore the assessment of participants' moral competence or even of their basic cognitive approaches to moral action. One way of clarifying the need for such assessment is to distinguish between beneficent and benevolent action. Beneficent action, that which benefits others, can have a variety of conceptual roots, many of them having nothing at all to do with charity and benevolence. The conceptual roots of benevolence, by contrast, lie in genuine love of the good of and for the sake of the other. Examining only a set of behavioral

4. A. L. Benton, A. B. Sivan, K. Hamsher, N. R. Varney, and O. Spreen, *Contributions to Neuropsychological Assessment* (New York: Oxford University Press, 1994), 35–52.

outcomes that are consistent with benefiting others will leave open the question of whether the behavior was due to rule-following, social desirability, expectation of reciprocal regard, or simply being in a giving mood. Cognitive modeling of behavior and/or conceptual structure from interviews, on the other hand, can go further in helping to assess whether a given model of valuational representation of self and other is driving the observed behaviors. For example, if researchers seek a neural systems model of compassion, it is unwise to simply proceed by linking action outcome with brain scans, and then to call whichever brain systems associate with outcomes benefiting others (i.e., beneficent action), systems for compassion. Prior to any neural model of compassion one first needs a cognitive model of compassion and a way to test for cognition according to that model. Such a model would be one that can be accessed and assessed by other scholars and rich enough in situated, naturalistic detail that it promises good external validity. Ideally, one's model of compassion would come in the form of existing persons or communities that are relatively easy to identify as compassionate. As Linda Zagzebski has noted, it is likely easier to reach agreement on moral categories across diverse cultural, social, and developmental contexts if the categories are embodied and come in the form of living examples, either of real persons or of rich, dramatic moral narratives on which a community's moral formation depends.[5]

Contrary to this thoughtful approach, moral averaging sidesteps the identification of putative exemplars and exemplary communities in action. If cognitive scientists who deny the importance of moral character and of empathy for the moral self rely heavily on evidence from moral averaging, it may not be so surprising when they report finding no such character, or that the entire notion is impossible. After all, much of the scientific work of moral averag-

---

5. L. T. Zagzebski, *Divine Motivation Theory* (Cambridge: Cambridge University, 2004), 347–88.

ing on which influential claims depend relies upon the thoughts, feelings, choices, and actions of populations in early adulthood (i.e., ages eighteen to twenty-two) whose moral motivations and identities are still labile and undergoing profound changes.[6]

Making Room for Human Action for a
Theologically Informed Virtue Science

There are three primary objections leveled against such a return to the phenomena in the form of putative exemplars and exemplary communities. First, there will be a theological suspicion that such focus on human action and agency impairs or imperils a full understanding of the function and work of grace. Grace, it is argued, is the beginning of the moral life—it comes from without and grasps or bathes the one graced, and it most certainly does not emerge from the typical developmental course of a community's moral growth or from the limited inter- and intrasubjective psychological processes at the core of that development. This challenge should not be minimized.

The notion that a turn toward exemplars and exemplarity imperils the place of grace may be most acutely felt among scholars seeking a deep engagement with Reformed theological ethics. Any response to this objection must resist the temptation to simply appropriate Roman Catholic virtue theoretic traditions, several of which are friendlier to a developmental approach that sees theological virtues as extensions of innate capacities. As Gerald McKenny insightfully observes in his deeply considered and excellent inquiry into Karl Barth's theological ethics, "If Protestantism has something of permanent importance to contribute to the universal church in

6. Tobias Krettenauer, Tyler Colasante, Marlis Buchmann, and Tina Malti, "The Development of Moral Emotions and Decision Making from Adolescence to Early Adulthood: A 6-Year Longitudinal Study," *Journal of Youth and Adolescence* 43 (2014): 583–96.

the field of moral theology, it is more likely to be found in Barth's reformulation of the Reformation tradition represented by Luther and Calvin than in [Protestant restatements of the Roman Catholic virtue theoretic traditions, which are typically] inferior versions of [rigorously developed] positions preserved and cultivated in the Catholic tradition."[7] Still, McKenny also affirms and explores recent developments in Barth scholarship that hold a key place for human activity in the moral life and contextualize that activity in the ongoing continuity of moral community:

> We have seen that Barth shares with casuistical ethics an orientation to the particular situation of choice or decision as central to ethics. He thereby opposes a kind of abstraction he finds in forms of ethics that operate only at the level of general principles. We have also seen that he avoids the opposite abstraction, in which the moment of choice or decision is considered independently of the continuous series of choices and decisions that form one's life. Ethical reflection involves "the examination [*Prüfung*] of the choice now before us in its connection with past and future choices" and our present deeds are always accompanied by the examination (*Prüfung*) of the will of God with respect to prospective deeds.[8]

So even Barth's overwhelming emphasis on the wholly divine approach of grace does not eclipse entirely the call to ethical reflection and examination within a contextual history. Surely, much more needs to be done in the area of action theories and Reformed theologies of grace, in the spirit of this volume. For now, it is enough to note that attending to the practices of morally salient communities and the persons formed by them need not be seen as a denial of any primary reality of grace. To the contrary, such attention to

---

7. Gerald McKenny, *The Analogy of Grace: Karl Barth's Moral Theology* (New York: Oxford University Press, 2010), 292.

8. McKenny, *The Analogy of Grace*, 275–76.

the lived practice of grace may help shape productive expressions of how grace comes to grasp these communities.

A second objection to the phenomenal turn within new approaches to theological inquiry into the moral life inevitably questions whether highlighting any given person's or community's example as *exemplary* undermines the very example under inquiry. This challenge must also be affirmed and accepted by those invested in new approaches to theological inquiry that are simultaneously humble and hopeful. The problematics of "exemplarity" as a source of insight in moral inquiry include the degree to which pluralistic cultures might uniformly embrace examples under this category, a general practical problem noted in the opening essay. Even more difficult, at least from a theoretical perspective, is the so-called "exemplar paradox," wherein those communities and persons seen as most exemplary of moral perception and wisdom often deny their own status as exemplars and include themselves among those most in need of transformation.[9] Traditionally, putative "exemplary" communities grounded in either the Dharmic or Abrahamic traditions resist and even strenuously deny any role as exemplar, pointing instead to the source(s) of transcendent experience, insight, wisdom, and virtue. It is easy to recall, for example, the numerous occasions upon which the Dalai Lama, questioned about his own contemplative and religious practices, has stated explicitly that he does not at all know how to meditate, and is still very much a person in formation in the Tibetan tradition. Similarly, Father Thomas Keating has repeatedly remarked, in public and private conversations, that he rejects any attempt to lift him above everyday contemplative practitioners of the Centering Prayer practice of which he is a recognized expert teacher. His instantiation of the exemplar paradox is even more puzzling when one considers that he reports that he no longer requires practicing Centering Prayer, since he is

9. Peterson et al., "The Rationality of Ultimate Concern." See also Mother Teresa, *Come Be My Light: The Private Writings of the Saint of Calcutta* (Colorado Springs: Image, 2007), 171–72.

now able by a simple consenting turn to accept the intimate embrace of the divine presence.

Finally, Jean Vanier and the leaders and assistants in the L'Arche communities around the world routinely deny any special status regarding their calling and work among adults with profound neuro-developmental disorders; instead, the emphasis is on the special gift that is the provenance of the core members, those superficially seen as disabled, but who are in reality the beauty of humanity in its full form. This view denying more familiar philosophical understandings of virtuous exemplarity is itself exemplified by Vanier's denial of generosity in favor of his affirmation of becoming a friend to others:

> When people are generous they are in control. You can imagine someone in the street falling down and you going to help that person to get up. Then something happens. As you listen to that person you become friends. Perhaps you discover that he or she is living in squalor and has little money. You are not just being generous, you are entering into a relationship, which will change your life. You are no longer in control. You have become vulnerable; you have come to love that person. You have listened to her story. You have been touched by that incredible, beautiful person who has lived something incredibly difficult. You are no longer in control, you are no longer just the generous one, you have become vulnerable. You have become a friend.[10]

These challenges remind us that in calling communities and persons of inspiring example *exemplary*, we risk contradicting one of the insights that we seek to understand and to guide our inquiry. Rather than recoiling from this risk and letting it prevent a return to the phenomena, however, we are called to become mindful of the risk. Seeking a constant mindfulness of this risk, allowing these

---

10. Jean Vanier, *Encountering the Other* (Dublin: Veritas, 2005), 37–39.

exemplary objections to orient the inquiries we undertake, we take the lessons of these phenomena—person and community—quite seriously. Our inquiry, instead of aiming solely and ending at the descriptively complex observables, will need to renew itself in a reorientation to the transcendent source to which the phenomena point and around which these persons and communities—by their own adamant claims—are formed. This is a reminder that our inquiries do not stop at an isolated, insular *habitus* embodied by the exemplar. Instead, our orientation must extend to that transcendent reality/experience toward which the exemplar points, and to the experiences and practices of *imitatio* that give an embodied moral life its form. One image of such inquiry is perhaps captured in the sixteenth-century painting done by Matthias Grünewald for the Isenheim Altarpiece, showing John the Baptist pointing at Jesus Christ on the cross. Grünewald's depiction included the famous words attributed to the Baptist in John's Gospel: "He must increase, I must decrease." The words of the Gospel writer do not refer to historical personages and their relative social and historical ranks. Instead, the envisioned juxtaposition is about ways of being in the world, about the transformation of self for and in the moral life. Grünewald's image, which Karl Barth raised above his writing desk, can serve to remind us regarding the exemplary communities central to our phenomenal turn that they are themselves formed in their *habitus* by an immersion in *imitatio* in transcendent relation. Every hope exists that reorienting virtue science toward the phenomena of exemplarity in this way might generate productive new models of human virtue and of human nature.

A third challenge must also be taken seriously, though it is not as helpful as the previous two. This challenge is also more obvious, within both theological and scientific approaches grounded in a view of human nature as individualistic, egoistic, concerned only with valuing the separated self, obsessed with self-gratification and aggrandizement, and deprived of any constitutive forms of fellowship. This challenge arises to say, in response to any interdisciplinary effort to focus—theologically, scientifically—on the living phenomena that are those persons and communities of long-term, dedicated, and morally salient life, the following: that while such inquiry may be interesting, it does little to help us understand the reality of human nature. In this challenge we face the objection that exemplars are not just temporal outliers, but outliers on the margins of humanity. They are not normal, not neurotypical, persons. To focus on the outliers, in other words, is ultimately unhelpful to the desired descriptive accounts of how morality works among the rest of us.

Sadly, this challenge is grounded in perspectives that only seem to be driven by the real-world phenomena on a large scale, but that in reality substitute ideology for a sensitivity to phenomenal life. Those who marginalize the importance of exemplary communities and persons for understanding the moral life seemingly privilege concepts like "typical," "normal," "everyday," "natural" ethics/ morality. The apparent descriptive scope of these terms belies the dependence of these viewpoints on a theoretical outlook committed to advocating narrow ethical self-interest and individualism over other possibilities. Of course, it may be the case that outlier communities, examples of the moral life that continue to inspire, resemble only faintly the broad sectors of human society in terms of transcendent, normative orientations, cultural and social commitments, developmental histories, psychological and neural systems, and even perhaps, most reductively speaking, of genetic makeup. What is often not acknowledged by the advocates of individualistic/ egoistic humanity—expressed very forcefully in the models *homo economicus*[11] and *homo rationalis*[12]—is their firm conviction about the genetic programming of human life for self-interest, aggression, violence, and domination, a conviction that is not supported by a

---

11. C. F. Camerer and E. Fehr, "When Does 'Economic Man' Dominate Social Behavior?," *Science* 311 (2006): 47–52.

12. Robert Aumann and Sergiu Hart, "An Interview with Robert Aumann," *Macroeconomic Dynamics* 9 (2005): 683–740.

careful review of primate and hominin evolution.[13] By extension, these advocates affirm genetic determinism regarding the scope and range of human moral development. These views form a collection of bio-ideologies decreeing no possible relevance of understanding morally exemplary "outliers" for the "typical" genetically endowed, because exemplars are biologically so different as to make any type of developmental and educational formation incapable of leading toward such atypical moral lives. To show how strong a hold this view exerts on the scientific community, even scientifically minded advocates of meditative practices—ostensibly practices that only make sense for a human nature capable of being transformed—can fall prey to its reductive genetics. They even go so far as to support a eugenicist program of moral transformation to breed new Buddhas.[14]

Consider instead the witness of exemplary persons and communities that there is no clear line of demarcation between those who belong to the supposed "outlier" communities and the rest of us. After all, if we listen to perspectives from those we tentatively identify as exemplars, they are us. Even more, to hear them tell of their struggles and transgressions in the moral life, they come across as sounding worse than more "typical" persons regard themselves. So a response to the "outlier" challenge that takes full account of the perspectives of exemplary communities will show this challenge to

13. Agustín Fuentes, "It's Not All Sex and Violence: Integrated Anthropology and the Role of Cooperation and Social Complexity in Human Evolution," *American Anthropologist* 106 (2004): 710–18.

14. "One can at least imagine a new era when some religious group within a culture might decide that it needed to raise and train a new leader. By then, the ancient custom of searching all over the world would long have been given up. And by then, 'reincarnation' would finally be appreciated as something determined solely by the laws which govern the human genome. In this far-distant era, it might then be realized that the desired child could best be conceived in a test tube and nurtured in a surrogate mother. Entering into the ever-braver union would be the ovum donated perhaps by a virginal nun, plus the sperm from an exemplary monk, both of whom had been screened and selected on the basis of their outstanding lineage and capacity." J. H. Austin, *Zen and the Brain* (Cambridge, MA: MIT, 1998), 689–90.

have no lasting force outside of a moral eugenics, or an inflexible, ideological commitment to atomism and egoism at the core of human being, genetically or socially constructed.

Imitatio and *Habitus*: Intentional I of a Self That Is Not Mine

Can there be a cognitive scientific approach that attends to the phenomena—to those persons and communities that provide inspiration and hope of moral transformation—while at the same time engaging directly with the challenge of grace? The remainder of this essay will suggest directions to pursue, directions whose discernment was only made possible through thorough critiques from colleagues at the Center of Theological Inquiry, though the remaining errors are my own.

To put forward a positive response to the first challenge discussed above, which denies a compatibility between exemplarity and grace, means an inquiry into *imitatio* and *habitus*, two core elements in moral theologies emerging from the Abrahamic traditions. In line with the mindfulness needed to meet the second challenge considered above, it is critical to attend closely to the self-understanding of *imitatio* among the exemplary communities that serve as the key phenomenal, experiential loci for our understanding. Ultimately, our attention requires that we be partners in conversation, listening closely to and partaking in the communities that inspire. For this paper, the written testimony of such communities will need to suffice.

We have already heard from one group of practitioners of friendship, through the witness of Jean Vanier writing about the L'Arche communities. Consider also the real-world community of forgiveness and reconciliation that is Homeboy Industries and the Homegirl Café, in downtown Los Angeles, California. These organizations are an outgrowth of Delores Mission Church, with a core spirituality emerging from the Society of Jesus, as expressed through the Jesuit spirituality of that community and of Father Gregory Boyle, who cofounded Homeboy.[15] Homeboy was founded for the sake of finding new life with rival gang members, women and men, many of whom have seen one another only as enemies.

When Boyle writes of Homeboy's impossible mission of creating kinship between and among people who literally may have sought to kill one another, his lesson is the lesson of *imitatio*: "Certainly, a place like Homeboy Industries is all folly and bad business unless the core of the endeavor seeks to imitate the kind of God one ought to believe in. In the end, I am helpless to explain why anyone would accompany those on the margins were it not for some anchored belief that the Ground of all Being thought this was a good idea."[16] What is notably absent in Boyle's language of *imitatio* on the way to realizing such kinship is any trace of saint-consciousness, any emphasis of the *I* who can competently explain to the rest of the world the "folly" that is his life's work. This *I* is not present, leaving only the *I* that cannot counter folly, that is helpless to explain except insofar as one's own becoming a friend to the others is grounded in the very transcendent divine whose mind conceived such accompaniment to begin with, and called it good.

Boyle expresses a clear rejection of any notion that this commitment of community has its origin and life in the self-made capacities of the committed. Instead of using a language stressing *I*-ness, he expressly uses the language of second-person address, a language of invitation to an aspirational community centered on and in and by a transcendent reality, with a perspective outside of any typical human point of view:

> Homies seem to live in the zip code of the eternally disappointing, and need a change of address. To this end, one hopes (against all human inclination) to model not the "one false move" God

15. Gregory Boyle, *Tattoos on the Heart: The Power of Boundless Compassion* (New York: Free Press, 2010), 73.
16. Boyle, *Tattoos on the Heart*, 21.

but the "no matter whatness" of God. You seek to imitate the kind of God you believe in, where disappointment is, well, Greek to Him. You strive to live the black spiritual that says, "God looks beyond our fault and sees our need."[17]

Living as such a person means embodying acceptance of others—*against all human inclination*—to put on the "no matter whatness" of divine perspective, to see only beauty and promise in the need of others. Boyle's view of Homeboy is a living community in which *imitatio* is not the work of a solitary saint or seeker, but that cultivates a communion with the divine mind, of a divine vision and embrace, an acceptance in the most dire circumstances of need. Boyle's placement of the *against* in his passage—"against all human inclination"—signals the depth of the antipathy to any striving exemplarity that stresses individual or even collective human capacity, absent transcendent relation.

This grace-filled grounding in transcendent encounter is perhaps more evident in Boyle's theology of compassion as *imitatio* of the love of God. Rejecting notions of compassion that restrict it to a "fleeting occasional emotion rising to the surface like eros or anger,"[18] he says instead that compassion is an aspect of community and that it must grow to vastness if humans are to embody its transcendent source and ultimate purpose: "If we long to be in the world who God is, then, somehow, our compassion has to find its way to vastness."[19] If even *hope* of being a model of boundless compassion is against all human inclination, as Boyle said above, then the modeling itself must itself not be identified with any typically salutatory inclination grounded in the human. So much is this modeling separate from human inclination that the *I* does not direct a compassion that is under its own control, its ownership. Compassion is *ours*, in Boyle's inclusive first-person plural possessive, not

17. Boyle, *Tattoos on the Heart*, 52.
18. Boyle, *Tattoos on the Heart*, 63.
19. Boyle, *Tattoos on the Heart*, 66.

mine. Compassion is not a trait or a quality of an individual person; it inheres in the community, not the individual, and then only insofar as the community expresses divine encounter, an expression of a self-with-others that eclipses the self of individualism and of in-group concerns.

We encounter in Boyle's language of *imitatio* a denial of familiar concepts generally associated in moral theology and philosophy with the term(s) habit/*habitus*, including concepts of inclination, disposition, trait, driving, striving, and saintliness. Boyle's *imitatio* has no *I* at the center, placing there instead the grace of transcendent encounter.

There is a similar movement away from striving and saintliness in the moral life in the later writings of Dietrich Bonhoeffer. In a letter to his dear friend Eberhard Bethge, Bonhoeffer contrasts the striving for saintliness with a desire to have faith:

> I remember a conversation I had thirteen years ago in America with a young French pastor. We had simply asked ourselves what we really wanted to do with our lives. And he said, I want to become a saint (—and I think it's possible that he did become one). This impressed me very much at the time. Nevertheless, I disagreed with him, saying something like: I want to learn to have faith. For a long time I did not understand the depth of this antithesis.[20]

Bonhoeffer raises themes in this letter, written the day after the failure of the July 20, 1944, attempt to kill Adolf Hitler, similar to those addressed by Boyle. Bonhoeffer is clearly uneasy with the way he portrayed saintliness in his book *Discipleship*, whose German title, *Nachfolge*, intentionally recalled the fifteenth-century work *Nachfolge Christi*, the *Imitation of Christ*, attributed to Thomas à Kempis.

---

20. Dietrich Bonhoeffer, *Letters and Papers from Prison* (Minneapolis: Fortress, 2009), 486.

In the summer of 1944, from Tegel Prison, Bonhoeffer reevaluated the book that he had completed only seven years before: "I thought I myself could learn to have faith by trying to live something like a saintly life. I suppose I wrote *Discipleship* at the end of this path. Today I clearly see the dangers of that book, though I still stand by it."[21] Instead of living a saintly life, Bonhoeffer's reflection is one of discovery, an ongoing realization about how thorough is faith's formation by the acceptance and the suffering of God. No longer should the faithful disciple be understood as "making something of oneself—whether it be a saint or a converted sinner . . . a just or unjust person, a sick or a healthy person." Faith means that one "throws oneself completely into the arms of God." For Bonhoeffer, faith is neither assent nor belief, neither attitude nor orientation, neither a mode of intention nor a comparative modeling, and, finally, it is not a forced imitation of Christ. Faith is when "one stays awake with Christ in Gethsemane," when "one takes seriously no longer one's own sufferings but rather the suffering of God in the world." Faith is a leap, to be sure, but a leap in which the *I* does not survive, to a place that saint-consciousness cannot go.

But doesn't Bonhoeffer contradict himself, since he clearly says that he looks to stay awake with Christ? Doesn't this mean that he places himself above the disciples who, after all, fell asleep? He does not enter into a contradiction if his "staying awake with Christ" is read as being taken up into the mind of Christ in the Garden, and being taken up into the suffering of Christ and God in the world, into a vast compassion. Then is the one waiting beside Christ making of herself the one who keeps awake, the disciple who would not sleep while the Master prayed? Bonhoeffer can be claiming no such role for himself, since he has already denied that striving and making "something of oneself" has anything to do with faith. Rather than saint-consciousness, what he calls for is keeping awake with Christ by being taken into an awareness—a being awake—that is the

---

21. Bonhoeffer, *Letters and Papers from Prison*, 486.

awareness and perspective of Christ praying in the Garden. Recall that when Christ finds the nearby disciples asleep, he pleads with them to stay awake, lest they fall into "temptation" (Matt. 26:41; Mark 14:38; Luke 22:46). The Greek word generally translated "temptation," *peirasmos*, is rooted in the verb *peiran*, which means "try," "attempt," "endeavor."[22]

Bonhoeffer knew this from his own reading of the Greek text. Staying awake, then, was not a matter of striving for him, but just its opposite. Three days before the letter of July 21, Bonhoeffer wrote to Bethge on the same theme:

> Being a Christian does not mean being religious in a certain way, making oneself into something or other (a sinner, penitent, or saint) according to some method or other. Instead it means being human, not a certain type of human being, but the human being Christ creates in us. It is not a religious act that makes someone a Christian, but rather sharing in God's suffering in the worldly life.[23]

In Bonhoeffer's understanding, the *metanoia* of faith, in which the community is "already shaped into the image of Christ . . . made like him" precedes any call to "again and again be 'like Christ' (καθὼς Χριστός)."[24] Once again Bonhoeffer places stress on being formed by the work of divine love, fashioned after the mind of divine love, prior to awakening to a *call*. The call is not a self-generated reminder or set of practices for isolated practitioners but an encounter that is only possible because of a participation that is already ongoing and with which the *I* had little to do. A participatory being "taken up" into the life and mind and love of the divine other is the meaning of *imitatio* in Bonhoeffer's renewed experience of being called to faith,

22. Walter Bauer, *A Greek-English Lexicon of the New Testament and Other Early Christian Literature* (Chicago: University of Chicago Press, 1957, 1979), 640–41.

23. Bonhoeffer, *Letters and Papers from Prison*, 480.

24. Dietrich Bonhoeffer, *Discipleship* (Minneapolis: Fortress, 2001 [1937]), 287.

an experience he relayed to his friend Bethge in the July 1944 letters. Boyle similarly addresses *imitatio* in terms of what he calls the "mystery" of becoming "locked onto the singularity of that love that melts you. It doesn't melt who you are, it melts who you are not."[25]

The ways in which both Boyle and Bonhoeffer interpret their experiences of *imitatio* can most readily be understood in terms of a theology of grace that embraces both exemplarity and the relational, constitutive transcendence at its source. Understanding *imitatio* in this way invites interdisciplinary inquiry into how *imitatio* may transform embodied persons and communities over time so that developmentally incremental or epiphanic changes stabilize and manifest more often in the consciousness and life of human communities. One place to begin a productive exploration of answers to this question is via new approaches to the concept of *habitus* in the work of Thomas Aquinas, along with its relation to the virtues in Thomistic moral theology. To understand Thomistic virtues requires an understanding of Thomistic *habitus*, since a virtue is a good *habitus* of the mind through which people "live righteously."[26] New approaches to theological inquiry into *habitus* require new theories of human deliberation and action, and so they may best proceed by including an engagement with contemporary sciences of valuation, emotion, decision, choice, and the sociovaluational constitution of the self. A full, constructive account along these lines is beyond the scope of this essay. Nevertheless, a useful start can be made by clarifying concepts and terms from decision science and theories of learning and memory that bear directly on the concepts that theologians use in new theological anthropologies regarding human choice and action, specifically relating to the struggle to define *habitus*. Terms from contemporary sciences of self-, valuation-, and decision-making should provide additional resources

25. Boyle, *Tattoos on the Heart*, 103.
26. Thomas Aquinas, *Summa theologiae* II–II, 55, 4. Thomas cites Augustine's definition of a virtue but changes Augustine's "quality of the mind" to "*habitus* of the mind": "si loco qualitatis habitus poneretur."

and metaphors for moral theology and possible connections for productive interdisciplinary work on moral formation.

Habitus and the Limits of Habituation

The choice of the familiar word "habit" to translate the Latin *habitus* in Thomas (and, by extension, the Greek *hexis* in Aristotle) is one of the primary obstacles in working with the notion of *habitus*. This difficulty is true both in moral theology and in the interdisciplinary endeavor that engages science. One problem of using "habit" to translate *habitus* is that it obscures multivalent uses of the terms *hexis* and *habitus* in their ancient and medieval contexts, sometimes in the same text. These multiple senses of *habitus* are poorly conveyed by the term "habit," leading more often than not to anachronisms arising in interpretation. Anachronistic tendencies stemming from the words "habit" and "habituation" come about because the words are strongly associated with mindless, automatic, and inflexible behaviors that lack all context sensitivity. Habits, in vernacular usage and in psychological theory, are often mere responses to particular triggers, no matter where those triggers appear or how they manifest. Someone with a smoker's habit, for example, does not experience a diminished urge to smoke when smoking is forbidden, say on an airplane or inside an office building. Unsurprisingly, the inadvisability of using habit and habituation has long been recognized by those most expert in the exposition of *habitus* in the work of Thomas Aquinas and its relevance for understanding the virtues for the moral life. In April 1960, Servais Pinckaers published a paper in *Nouvelle Revue Théologique* titled, "Virtue Is Not a Habit."[27] In the second volume of his magnum opus on the life and theology of Aquinas, Jean-Pierre Torrell notes that, for *habitus*,

---

27. Servais Pinckaers, "Virtue Is Not a Habit," *Cross Currents* (Winter 1962): 65–81, trans. Bernard Gilligan.

"We do not have a word in our modern languages to express exactly this central notion. We must thus keep *habitus*, but should avoid translating it as 'habit,' for this term suggests rather the contrary of the true meaning."[28] Romanus Cessario similarly rejects the concept of habit in arguing strongly for a view of *habitus* that is nothing like "an acquired pattern of behavior which results, principally, from repeated actions of the same kind, like putting so many creases in a starched linen cloth."[29]

The concerns raised by Pinckaers, Torrell, and Cessario should be taken quite seriously in efforts to interpret *habitus* and the virtues for moral theologies that seek to be open to interdisciplinary approaches with contemporary cognitive theories of valuation, choice, and action. The concerns are deeply conceptual, pitting the flexibility, context sensitivity, and choice inherent to *habitus* against the inflexibility, context insensitivity, and automaticity of habit. Given the serious nature of these problems and the scholarly standing of the moral theologians raising them, it is surprising that so many moral theologies nonetheless use the term *habit* to translate *habitus* but also interpret *habitus* by drawing on the repetitive automaticity and/or absence of choice that are aspects of habit.[30] This willingness to put up with the limitations of habit and habituation may be due in part to both a sense that contemporary scientific views of habit do not restrict one to automaticity and that contemporary scientific views of human valuation, choice, and action do not have other categories more suitable than habit. The actual situation within the affective and decision sciences is quite otherwise, and the present essay will conclude by offering a brief sketch that may help begin

28. Jean-Pierre Torrell, *Saint Thomas Aquinas*, vol. 2, *Spiritual Master* (Washington, DC: Catholic University of America Press, 2003 [1996]), 264.

29. Romanus Cessario OP, *The Moral Virtues and Theological Ethics* (Notre Dame: University of Notre Dame, 2009), 35.

30. Jennifer A. Herdt, *Putting On Virtue: The Legacy of the Splendid Vices* (Chicago: University of Chicago Press, 2008), 83, 246–47. David Decosimo, *Ethics as a Work of Charity: Thomas Aquinas and Pagan Virtue* (Stanford, CA: Stanford University Press, 2014), 74–76.

a move away from habit toward a richer conception of *habitus* for interdisciplinary work in the twenty-first century.

William James, a significant influence on psychological theory, defined habit in terms of habits of character that come about by frequent repetition, almost mindlessly transforming behavior in response to a particular trigger or idea. In his *Talks to Teachers*, he drew on his treatment of habit and character in *The Principles of Psychology* to say that character is "an organized set of habits of reaction," where habits are "tendencies to act characteristically when certain ideas possess us, and to refrain characteristically when possessed by other ideas."[31] Contemporary cognitive science and cognitive theory formulate habits as even more mindlessly automatic. On the view of cognitive science, habits are, fundamentally, and unlike *habitus*, not goal-directed behaviors. For an action to be goal-directed, there must be a learned association between an organism's response and the outcome of that response (i.e., "response-outcome control") and the expected outcome must align with motivation at the time of response. Habituated behaviors have nothing to do with either of these basic conditions. Habits are behaviors that are completely independent of an outcome's *current* value, and only depend on past, overlearned associations. Thus in contemporary cognitive science, habits are not sensitive to contextual changes, they are inflexible and are difficult to unlearn, and they are purely stimulus-response behaviors,[32] where the "stimulus" can be a complex context. Another way to frame habits is provided by the social psychologists Wendy Wood and David T. Neal, who state the two key principles that characterize habits this way: (1) "an outsourcing of behavioral control to context cues that were, in the past, contiguous with performance"; and (2) "performed without mediation of a goal to achieve a particular outcome or a goal to respond (i.e., a

---

31. William James, *Talks to Teachers on Psychology: And to Students on Some of Life's Ideals* (New York: Henry Holt & Co., 1899), 184.

32. Ray J. Dolan and Peter Dayan, "Goals and Habits in the Brain," *Neuron* 80 (2013): 312–25.

behavioral intention)."[33] They are, as the authors point out, "the residue of past goal pursuit," where the residue is free of any intention or sensitivity to context or sensitivity to outcome. These definitions are by no means outliers in the scientific field, but are almost universally understood when cognitive scientists theorize about habit learning, otherwise known as habituation.

Happily, those interested in drawing on contemporary cognitive theory for new models of *habitus* for understanding the moral life can look beyond theories of habit to theories of valuation and learning. There are several approaches within the cognitive science of learning that will be of use in future integrative inquiry into virtue formation. The first two may be more important for instrumental valuation during early formation of social norms and expectations, while the last may be important for making a transition to *habitus* required for the formation of virtue.

The first approach is that of reinforcement learning, which models a person's learning on the basis of relationships between different contexts, context-permitted responses, the response-dependent movement between contexts (i.e., response-dependent transition probabilities between contexts), and the outcome (i.e., reward/punishment) associated with each context. One can imagine a person perceiving a complex morally relevant situation involving many potential contexts, where each context has associated actions (i.e., responses), each action favors a move to another context that needs to be addressed, and each choice has a morally relevant outcome that is either beneficial or harmful. In so-called "model-free" learning, agents have no ability to "model" the complex set of transitions between contexts or to choose between them, but can only change their response after a given action based on the difference between their expected outcome and the actual outcome of that action. The cues that are most salient

---

33. Wendy Wood and David T. Neal, "A New Look at Habits and the Habit-Goal Interface," *Psychological Review* 114 (2007): 843–63.

for training are the rewards and punishments given in response to courses of action.

Contrast this lack of ability of "model-free" learning with "model-based" learning, which can represent a complex set of associated cues—putative morally salient characteristics of a given situation. Model-based learning, rather than responding on a trial-by-trial basis, allows agents to have the ability to form highly detailed plans involving numerous contexts, thereby enabling them to be sensitive enough to represent and choose actions that favor even small probabilities of positive outcome. In practice, model-based learning does much better at solving more complex learning tasks than does model-free learning, and its acquisition may be associated with maturation in development. Like *habitus*, but unlike habit, model-based learning is a stable ordering of salient cues—cues that could signal moral salience/significance—and potential outcomes. Like *habitus*, these cues are stable and can be themselves shaped in a context-sensitive manner via learning, a process that also includes choices. Yet there is still a problem with model-based learning that depends primarily on associating salient cues and their structure with rewards and punishments. Such a framework provides no way forward to relate *habitus* to *imitatio*, since the model in model-based reinforcement learning has no way of including an o/Other.

In order to represent and explicitly model beliefs that an agent has about another agent with whom she is interacting, it is necessary to draw on cognitive models that directly incorporate explicit representation of beliefs about what other agents believe. For, as Jennifer Herdt makes clear in her example of the little child and the kitten with whom the child needs to learn to play nicely, or in her example of a child learning to be virtuously generous rather than only acting as if she were generous to earn the approval of her elders, virtuous formation requires a way of choosing "for reasons characteristic of the virtuous."[34] Without a representation of the good of others

34. Herdt, *Putting On Virtue*, 25–26.

and of their own beliefs and desires about that good—not just in terms of one's own actions but in terms of valuing their standing and their own intentionality, autonomy, etc.—there will be no real formation of virtue, only the formation of social norms. Cognitive science and the field of mimetic robotics recently developed theoretic approaches that go beyond reinforcement learning by allowing representations of others independent of what the other is expected to do for or for the sake of the choosing agent. Although these directions are still very new and under intense development, one could imagine how a set of beliefs in agent A about agent G's beliefs about agent B could be represented, where agent G's beliefs are now the primary set of influences shaping future action choices on the part of agent A. Some of these complexities could even make use of simulation theories to suggest how an agent might be infused with the mind of G on B. Developments such as these may allow formal learning models both for how "striving" and of "staying awake with" the exemplar agent G affect subsequent learning and the kinds of actions and values that take effect and lead to further responses. There may be bi-stable transitions, in which agents abruptly shift from striving to awakening, or there may be more gradual shifts or multiply realizable stable agent configurations. In any case, having such formal models at hand for new approaches in moral theology is much more likely to yield models of virtuous formation than relying on models of habit and habituation, which only serve to block progress required for deep integrative engagement.

3

In the Divine (Mental) Image

Theological Anthropology and the Structures of Cognition

COLLEEN SHANTZ

In this essay the path of interdisciplinary theology wends its way from the particular to the general. The particular is, first, St. Paul, the self-described runt of the apostolic litter (1 Cor. 15:8), who nonetheless is equally well described as the first theologian of the Christ movement. Indeed, Paul articulated among the first Christological formulations (e.g., the first and second Adam, the kenotic Christ) and some of the most enduring psychagogic patterns in the tradition (e.g., death to self, flesh and spirit, *theōsis*). One extraordinary aspect of Paul's thinking is how deeply it is tied to religious experience. A sympathetic reader cannot fail to notice how much of Paul's knowledge he understands to have come from revelations: the impetus for his second trip to Jerusalem (Gal. 1:18), his visions of Christ (1 Cor. 15:8; 2 Cor. 3:18), and his message (Gal. 1:11–12; 2 Cor. 4:5–7). Paul's religious experience has been a research interest of mine for some time and comprised the heart of my project while at CTI. The interior character of experience poses a particular challenge for study. Thus, one specific of this interdisciplinary path is cognitive science, including evolutionary theory, and what it can help us to probe about the functioning and structure of the human mind. Indeed, the first part of this essay introduces some of this material. The second part considers ecstatic experience as a particular form of cognition that, although more rare than the others, is equally natural.

In the third part, the trail of inquiry broadens to more generalized questions of theological anthropology, especially as captured in the category of *imago Dei*. *Imago Dei* has never been a central doctrinal thread in the systematic tapestry. In part this may be due to its poetic character—it originates in the biblical creation account, which structures temporal and ontological categories into a mythic order with the human being, *ha'adam*, and the planet Earth at the center of the plot. Thus, in its original form, *imago Dei* is more naturally suited to theopoetics than systematics. Indeed, the concept of the divine image has probably played its strongest role in theologies of emancipation that responded to the slavery, the Shoah, and the diminishment of women and people with disabilities.

Still, throughout the centuries, Christian theologians have nominated a variety of attributes as that which carries the image: rationality, freedom of will, communication, a future-directed imagination, creativity, the capacity for worship. All of these nominees, as Celia Deane-Drummond suggests, "point to a different kind of mentalizing" than the rest of the animals exercise.[1] So, at least within Christian tradition human minds are consistently implicated in the discussion of what it might mean to bear the divine image. And certainly since Thomas Aquinas, it is the capacity for reasoning and intelligence that has dominated theological imagination in this regard. Interestingly, within Judaism, uninterrupted by a doctrine of original sin, human embodiment in itself has persisted as a potential bearer of the *imago Dei*.

---

1. Celia Deane-Drummond, *The Wisdom of the Liminal: Evolution and Other Animals in Human Becoming* (Grand Rapids: Eerdmans, 2014), 11. Interestingly, in its history of interpretation of the term, Judaism seems to have favored the categories of embodiment and morality.

Just as *imago Dei* is poorly calibrated for systematic theology, its origin in a narrative account of creation also makes it difficult to assimilate to scientific discourse. One point of divergence is their distinctive descriptions of human development: through teleology in the creation account as opposed to adaptation in evolutionary hypotheses. The biblical story of God's creation of humanity depicts a fixed ideal—distinguished from other animals and present from the beginning—from which humans have departed and to which we might be returned by God's grace. By contrast, the evolutionary principle of adaptation suggests change in response to conditions, which by definition cannot be directed to a predetermined end, but is contingent and reactive.

Clearly, *imago Dei* more easily accommodates teleological patterns than models of fitness-governed adaptation. But it is less clear that this match is based in deep consideration of the human mind, especially given the advances in brain studies in recent decades. In this essay I will explore the broad categories of the human mind as a kind of cognitive ecology whose adaptability bolstered its evolutionary advantage. Through close attention to the character of the human mind I hope we might uncover new possibilities for evolutionary theory and theology to instruct and improve one another. One of the surest ways to explore these questions is to listen deeply to both the theological witness (with special attention in this case to scripture) and the biological witness and to consider sympathetically their shared interests.

We begin with a slight academic-autobiographical detour before returning to the main path of the essay. The project that I pursued while a fellow at CTI concerns the (traditional) category of Paul's conversion. For a number of reasons I do not find "conversion" to be a useful, or even accurate, designation. For one thing, it requires that we privilege a somewhat uncritical reading of the idealized narratives in Acts over Paul's own accounts of his life. Second, the category of conversion is deeply invested in confessional ideologies, particularly the supremacy of Christianity but also the denigration of religious exuberance.[2] Despite the fact that there was no "Christianity" for Paul to convert to during his lifetime, he has served as the first symbolic convert from Judaism, a claim that implicitly fuels supersessionist theologies and, for that reason alone, should give us pause. But most significantly, important critiques of the category of conversion have been forwarded from several academic fronts that have convinced me of the need to use it with more caution. Sociologists have questioned its utility for naming the heart of the matter. What precisely does the application of the term help us to see? Surely, they have argued, the most significant datum attached to the concept is the movement of a subject from one group to another and that movement is a process, not a moment in time, and owes as much to the structure and function of groups as it does to any interior experience.[3] That early work has since been supported and elaborated by (social) psychologists who have studied conversion reports and elaborated on stages of change.[4]

Notwithstanding these legitimate hesitations, my current research on Paul is invested precisely in the debated interest in moments of dramatic religious experience. It is my contention that, having established so firmly the progressive nature of "conversion," we are now in a position to reassess the contribution of such experiential moments; for, although they are not sufficient to account for significant personal change, the people who undergo them consistently speak of their importance. We might do well to treat their self-reports seriously.

As mentioned, one obvious means to approach Paul's religious experience is through studies of the brain and cognition. Paul's let-

2. I discuss this range of ideological wrinkles in *Paul in Ecstasy: The Neurobiology of the Apostle's Life and Thought* (New York: Cambridge University Press, 2009), 20–66.

3. The watershed sociological work on conversion as a process is John Lofland and Rodney Stark, "Becoming a World-Saver: A Theory of Conversion to a Deviant Perspective," *American Sociological Review* 30, no. 6 (1965): 862–75.

4. The classic work in this category is Lewis Rambo's *Understanding Religious Conversion* (New Haven: Yale University Press, 1993).

ters make it clear that some of what he came to know was not by normal processes of reasoning. He also understands these insights to be of God, and thus refers to them as revelations or as signs and wonders. So, what might we learn by exploring as thoroughly as possible the mental character of such flashes of insight? If we accept the theological tradition, developed over time, that we bear the divine mental image, what might that, in turn, tell us about human and divine identity?

What Kind of Minds Do We Possess?

Of course the question in the heading is impossible to answer with anything approaching thoroughness. Instead this section loosely maps the range of our cognition through triangulation with each point illustrated primarily by a single (set of) author(s). The three points in the survey are (1) dual-process theory, (2) parallel process theory, and (3) meaning-maintenance theory. Aspects of all three will seem familiar given that we experience them daily; however, the extent to which nonconscious processing functions in each is somewhat surprising. Nonetheless the studies underway in these areas are helping to further define the workings of our minds. After establishing these foundational details we can consider another mode of processing—the sort implicated in religious experience.

As we work our way through an average day, our thinking typically proceeds along an efficient division of labor, often called Type 1 and Type 2. Nobel laureate and behavioral economist Daniel Kahneman is widely associated with this theory even though he was not the first to elaborate it. He describes our quick, Type 1 thinking as ideally suited to address the external, material world with maximal efficiency. Much of its content is accumulated through experience but once it is learned, the source and construction of the knowledge becomes invisible to us. Furthermore, Kahneman illustrates the automatic nature of Type 1 knowledge by observing that "you cannot prevent yourself from understanding sentences in your own language," or from knowing the answer to a simple arithmetic question, discerning hostility in someone's voice, or thinking of the capital of your own country when asked.[5]

These are all Type 1 responses. In contrast, Type 2—deliberate, effortful, conscious thinking—is employed in more complex computations like three-digit multiplication, the choice between two health insurance plans, crossing the street at a busy intersection, or behaving appropriately at a formal dinner. The two types interact throughout our waking hours with the degree of focus shifting between them; however, Type 2 tends to be reserved for the unfamiliar or the difficult, situations that demand more resources in order to be resolved. When I process things in this second mode I am aware of myself as a thinker and my cognition feels like an expression of self.

Dual-processing theories suggest a lot about the automaticity of some cognition and, concomitantly, about the way it can proceed without our awareness. But they do not describe all the ways our minds function, even with regard to conscious and nonconscious processing. In fact, there are more layers and complexities between conscious and unconscious cognition than the term *dual* process implies. One interesting and frequently cited example of another sort of thinking—embodied cognition—is the case of an outfielder catching a fly ball. She does not do so by consciously calculating where the ball will land and placing herself there in advance, but by moving laterally while simultaneously adjusting her speed of motion relative to the trajectory of the ball. Because of her movements the ball appears, within her field of vision, to remain stationary and she is ideally situated to catch it. The successful catch requires an effortful focus on the ball but also the unconscious embodied cognition that automatically guides the fielder's speed and position.

5. Daniel Kahneman, *Thinking, Fast and Slow* (Toronto: Doubleday Canada, 2011), 22.

If a player were to interrupt his unconscious responses in order to consciously assess the movements of the ball and consciously think about his placement relative to them, the catch would be much more difficult to complete.

Notwithstanding additional complexities, the model of two types has significant explanatory power. Kahneman's interest in distinguishing them grew out of his observations that Type 1 does not always serve us well in decision-making. We regularly make statistical errors based on Type 1's readymade heuristics. So, although these modes evolved as the most efficient use of intellectual energy and although they serve us well for the majority of cognitive tasks that we face, they are far from flawless.

As Antonio Damasio so pithily suggests, "our brains know more than our conscious minds reveal." That hidden surplus has been explored since around the middle of the twentieth century, when studies of so-called split-brain patients provided some of the earliest evidence to hint at the degree of suppressed knowledge. These patients had severe and intractable epilepsy. So damaging were their symptoms that in some cases surgeons severed the patient's corpus callosum (the dense series of neural fibers that connect the brain's right and left hemispheres) in order to confine the electrical damage of seizures to only one side of the brain. The surgery achieved its immediate purpose but it also initiated changes in the patients' behavior. A few of these cases famously illustrated that the brain's right and left hemispheres often function with distinct purposes—indeed, virtually two independent sets of consciousness resulted. For example, one man was observed repeatedly pulling off his pants with his left hand and pulling them back up with his right. These studies also helped to identify hemispheric specialization, including the sometimes-conflicting motivations that drive the various systems.

This conflict among neural and endocrine systems is aptly illustrated by the example of "romantic" love. The experience of love comprises three separate systems (see the table on p. 57), each with its own chemical fingerprint, motivations, and associated behaviors. Initial fMRI studies support the likelihood that each system draws on distinctive and consistent neural groupings as well.[6]

	Sex-Drive	Attraction	Attachment
Evolutionary function	mating	reproduction	nesting/territory protection
Neurochemical distinctiveness	estrogens & androgens	dopamine, norepinephrine (decreased serotonin)	oxytocin & vasopressin
Adaptive advantage	facilitates sexual union with all possible mates	conserves mating energy by identification of preferable match	Increases effectiveness of parenting through cooperative effort

Each of these systems provides a distinct reproductive advantage within a discrete ecological context directed toward a particular aspect of sexual selection. For example, where the number of potential mates is significantly constrained, group members who were predisposed to mate as widely as possible were more likely to be successful and hence to pass on their lust-facilitating genes to offspring. In cases of more abundant mate selection (and possibly some competition among one sex or the other) the attraction system is thought to facilitate the most successful reproduction by fixating the mater's energies on the most genetically viable partner. For its part, the attachment system directs energies toward the survival of resulting offspring and provides a survival advantage in situations of threats from outside of the kin group. Thus, each of these drives participates in sexual selection but does so in a distinctive way, producing different motivations, behavior and, hence, distinctive cognitive patterns.

6. Helen E. Fisher, Arthur Aron, Debra Mashek, Haifang Li, and Lucy L. Brown, "Defining the Brain Systems of Lust, Romantic Attraction, and Attachment," *Archives of Sexual Behavior* 31, no. 5 (2002): 413–19. The article discusses the neuroimaging study as well as other information in this subsection.

They run independently of one another, in parallel. Furthermore, nothing inherent in these three systems brings them into harmony within a human agent; indeed, by their nature they often generate cross-purposes. Evolutionary biologist David Haig describes how such conflicts go all the way down to the level of our genes.[7] In part this is due to the fact that we inherit half of our genes from each parent and these genes were sometimes selected in ecosystems that were remarkably different from one another.

One further negative upshot of such parallel systems—and there are other examples—is that we often feel fragmented, and various idioms express this state: "I am of two minds about it" or "I do not know my own mind." Who is the "I" that is separate from the thinking in "I can't make up my mind"?

The third point of triangulation comprises the confusion of goals and behaviors that sometimes arise from this mix of conscious and unconscious cognition along with independently functioning biological drives. Travis Proulx describes a wide-ranging set of experiments conducted over the past twenty to thirty years that have been designed to probe this confusion. Most of the studies begin by threatening some aspect of subjects' meaning schemas and then "give them the opportunity to 'fluidly compensate' for whatever it is that our threat manipulation has just drained away."[8] The experiments have used threats to self-esteem, to identity and belonging, and to effective personal agency. Proulx argues that a single psychological mechanism lies behind these diverse contexts, that "a common resource is being depleted." That resource is meaning. But these abstract principles are more comprehensible with an example.

In one ingeniously designed experiment,[9] Proulx and Steven

7. David Haig, "Intrapersonal Conflict," in *Conflict*, ed. Martin Jones and A. C. Fabian (New York: Cambridge University Press, 2006), 8–22.

8. Travis Proulx, "Threat-Compensation in Social Psychology: Is There a Core Motivation?" *Social Cognition* 30, no. 6 (2012): 643–51, 645.

9. Travis Proulx and Steven J. Heine, "The Case of the Transmogrifying Ex-

Heine recruited a group of undergrads, ostensibly to engage them in responding to various surveys. The design involved three experimental groups: A, the control group; B, the death-salience group; and C, the changing-experimenter group. All three sets of subjects began by answering a neutral survey about their entertainment preferences. Group A was immediately instructed to read a "hypothetical report about the arrest of a prostitute" after which they had to determine the amount of the bond for her release as if they were the judge in the case. Following the initial survey, members of Group B answered two questions about their own death before completing the arrested prostitute study. Finally, while Group C was completing the entertainment questionnaire, their experimenter was surreptitiously replaced by another, identically dressed, but physically quite a different person. The few participants who noticed the change were removed from the study. The remaining subjects moved on to the task of setting the bond for the fictitious prostitute.

The point of the study was to see whether stimulation of the threat of death (Group B) or disruption of perceptual schemas (Group C) made any difference in the amount set for the bond. It did. In the end, the students under the changing-experimenter condition judged the prostitute more severely by setting significantly higher bond rates than the control group. So too did the students whose awareness of their own deaths was stimulated (not to the same degree but the difference between B and C fell within the margin of error). What is most remarkable about these differences is what Proulx describes as "the radical substitutability of one meaning framework for another following a meaning threat."[10] In other words, although the arrest of the prostitute has no logical relationship to a vague sense of something not quite being right with the experimenter, it nonetheless provides a means to compensate for the loss of meaning for the subject. By asserting greater control

perimenter: Affirmation of a Moral Schema Following Implicit Change Detection," *Psychological Science* 19, no. 12 (2008): 1294–1300.

10. Prouxl and Heine, "The Case of the Transmogrifying Experimenter," 1295.

over the legal/moral circumstances in the story the students counteracted some of the loss of perceptual control in the lab—even
when they were not conscious that it was bothering them!

Together the three sets of studies mark out some of the parameters of the complex workings of our minds. We frequently rely
on heuristics that are unexamined, we contend with biological and
behavioral drives that are in conflict within any given scenario, and
our behavior and choices are motivated by goals of which we are
unaware and that are not fully aligned. We are opaque, even to
ourselves. These conditions raise questions about the coherence of
identity, action, and values; about the psychic toll of subconscious
conflicts; and about the ability to choose wisely and with integrity.
Paul's speech-in-character in Romans 7:21–24 captures the fragmentation well:

> So then, I find that while my desire is to do what is right, that
> which is wrong lies alongside. For I share delight in the law of
> God in my inner self, but I see a different law in my parts, war
> ring against the law of my mind and captivating me by the law
> of sin that is in my parts. How wretched a human being I am!
> Who will deliver me from this body of death?

Ecstatic Knowing

The sort of consciousness undertaken in religious experience differs in significant ways from the patterns just described through
triangulation. In brief, it is characterized by gestalt cognition, by
integration of emotion, by self-transcendence, and by a sense of the
numinous. In addition, it appears to be a capacity that was present
relatively early in our evolution, and theories about its appearance
vary (viz., whether the trait was naturally selected or is an exaptation or even a merely curious by-product). Of course there are experiences of altered consciousness that are connected with chronic

neurochemical imbalances, seizures, or brain injury; however, some ecstatic experiences arise from the ordinary capacities of the nervous system functioning in extraordinary ways. Furthermore, while precise distinctions between phenomena may be debated, it would be pedantic to argue that there is no category of healthy ecstatic experience. Indeed, many cultures throughout history have cultivated and depended upon ecstatic practices for a variety of functions.

That Paul underwent more than one such shift in consciousness is clear from his own letters. He describes a number of occasions of ecstatic experience in his life. His ascent to the "third heaven" (2 Cor. 12:1–4) and the description of his vision of the face of Christ (2 Cor. 3:12–18) are two striking examples. He also attributes his call to the Gentiles to such an experience: "But when God, who had set me apart from my mother's womb and called me by his grace, was pleased to reveal his Son in me, in order that I might preach him among the Gentiles, immediately I did not confer with anyone" (Gal. 1:15–16). The phrase "to reveal his son *in me*" pithily encapsulates the experience. Interestingly—and dubiously—most English translations render this as "reveal his son *to me*," obscuring the interiority of the religious experience (and aligning it more closely with the account in Acts).

Ecstatic experiences are frequently characterized by the emotion of awe or wonder; indeed, often the emotion is the sole factor of analysis. But this emotion (indeed all emotions) also has cognitive content. On the basis of a literature review and a series of experiments that probed the character of awe, Dacher Keltner and Jonathan Haidt concluded that awe comprises the twofold appraisal of: (1) "perceived vastness" and (2) the drive to accommodate the stimulus.[11] Often, with the passage of time, people are able to articulate more propositional content associated with the experience, but such formulations are typically not the primary shape that the

11. Dacher Keltner and Jonathan Haidt, "Approaching Awe, a Moral, Spiritual, and Aesthetic Emotion," *Cognition & Emotion* 17, no. 2 (March 2003): 297–314.

experience takes. Indeed, it is the phenomenology of self-transcendence and the utterly compelling nature of the experience that seem most salient initially. The cognitive structure of awe thus tends to exceed existing boundaries and categorization and to drive the subject to accommodate more expansive framing. Insight of this sort is a common—nearly constituent—feature of ecstatic experiences.

In Paul's case, his "call" is accompanied by the insight, also recorded in the letter to the Galatians, that "there is no more Judean or Hellenist, nor is there slave or free, nor male and female, for you are all one in Christ Jesus" (Gal. 3:28). Further, it was this revelation/recognition that impelled him from that point on. I want to pause a moment over the character of Paul's insight because it was one of those extraordinary theological breakthroughs that changes the course of a movement. As the philosopher Alain Badiou describes it, Paul articulates freedom from both the (state or cultural) overdetermination of even our most mundane choices, on the one hand, and, on the other hand, from the extraordinary indeterminacy of human potential—or, as Badiou puts it, the "pure contingency of multiple-being."[12] This psychobiological indeterminacy is the Charybdis to the Scylla of culture. In Paul's context, ethnicity and social status comprised the overdetermined aspect of identity. Paul escapes this rigid contextualization of religious-ethnic identity by appeal to a universal humanity made possible by the transformation of resurrection. Likewise, he transcends the embodied fragmentation and indeterminacy of the human condition by claiming an identity.

For heuristic purposes we might consider insight of this sort as a third type of cognition. We might even, with a certain degree of license, call it Type 3 in order to distinguish its patterns of conscious and nonconscious cognition from Types 1 and 2. Like Type 1, this form of cognition is emotionally coherent and the bulk of its work is done behind the veil of consciousness. Like system 2 its resulting

---

12. Alain Badiou, *Saint Paul: The Foundation of Universalism* (Stanford, CA: Stanford University Press, 2003), 4.

ideas tend to be complex, integrative of a wide range of issues, and reflective of a high level of abstraction. Insight does not seem to be effortful and its content is not always propositional even when it is meaningful. The knowledge that arises in this third way is novel as opposed to familiar but deeply connected to circumstances with which the individual is engaged. Further, ecstatic insight is generally more emotionally intense and rich and the subject's sense of its veracity or at least its significance tends to be stronger than through other ways of knowing. Some of these characteristics pertain more to phenomenology than epistemology but this does not diminish their significance.

The misalignment in our meaning-making systems can be psychologically disruptive to individuals, but sometimes it is disruptive even at the level of larger social structures. Indeed, religious insight seems to occur often in periods of meaning stresses. Ethnographic studies suggest that ecstatic practices are characteristically associated with complex societies (politically hierarchical, in relationships with neighboring states or jurisdictions, and internally stratified) and that they appear most frequently in periods of social turmoil and renewal. Cities within the Roman Empire in the first century CE are perfect examples of these conditions. Such circumstances are costly in social and psychological capital. They require rich contextual information if members of these societies are to navigate relationships successfully. I sometimes apply the computer term *defragging* as metaphor for these insight experiences. Defragmentation of a computer is the process of reuniting the data of a file that have become physically separated and distributed across a hard drive, thus slowing its processing. In defragmentation, files are reconstituted in ways that facilitate the more effective functioning of a computer's design. Paul's resolution of the nature of God with the universality of humanity was one such social realignment. Thus, ecstatic insight might be equated to a kind of biological-cultural wisdom practice.

Imago Dei and the Evolved Mind

To repeat the claim at the beginning of this essay, this final section will reflect on *imago Dei* in light of this more detailed examination of human cognition. Given the general consensus that human mind is the most fitting aspect to bear the divine image, what insights arise from the slower, more detailed examination of the character of the human mind? Here I will sketch three that might function as starting points for more thorough consideration.

In my introductory comments I referred to the cognitive ecology of human cognition. We are now in a position to consider that ecology more fully. Our cognitive systems seem to be adaptive partly because they facilitate a kind of processing triage. Type 1 responds to circumstances that we encounter frequently. Its processing reflects the effects of millennia of interaction with the environment, including other agents. It deploys whole sets of evolved heuristics that are well suited for quick responses to potential threats and advantages in the immediate environment. It also relies, in part through affectivity, on the associations that a person builds through experience. But Type 1 heuristics produce errors in more complex or unusual situations. (Indeed, Kahneman formed his theories through analysis of common errors in statistical judgments.) Type 2 compensates for some of this bias, allowing us to temper not only cognitive heuristics but also biological drives and affective associations, in part by facilitating the integration of cultural norms. Further still, Type 3 seems able to generate paradigm shifts when a system becomes so imbalanced that it no longer functions effectively for social groups. Religious insight provides a means not only of insight, but also of the kind of emotional and convictional coherence that enables one to integrate behavior with ideas.

One of the most remarkable characteristics of human mentalizing is its deep and thorough materiality. This claim exceeds the simple observation that our brains are composed of cells—that they are fleshly, as Paul might put it. Rather, it is the recognition that human cognition depends upon embeddedness in the environment, including the interaction with other minds. The genetically encoded elements of Type 1 thinking are the traits that were selected precisely because they facilitated meaningful interaction with the material world. Thus, our ability to reason, to build knowledge, to test and adapt it is inseparable from embodiment. Our cognition is distributed—throughout our bodies, across the gathered minds that interact in any social setting, even across our own history of accumulated experience. Without bodies, a material world, other humans, our minds would not be recognizable. There is no reason without the stuff upon which it operates.

What and who we are is realized in this dynamic manifestation rather than through arrival at a finished state. Many implications arise from this recognition: regarding ontology, the inherently social or permeable nature of human being; regarding ideology, the cultural exaggeration of individuality; regarding metaphysics, the inextricability of spirit and matter in the capacity of cognition. What does this suggest of the divine image? Certainly it points away from neo-Platonic views of the divine mind or other constructions that denigrate the real in favor of the ideal. It sits more comfortably with the suggestion that the *imago Dei* subsists in our capacity for communion. Indeed, in the case of human cognition communion (interchange or interpenetration) is not merely a capacity; rather it is actually constitutive. It is not that cognition is dependent on the material or impeded by it, but that materiality is within its essence.

The next two points are closely related, the first addressing primarily theological constructions and the second directed toward evolutionary theory. One of the striking features about the evolution of our minds is its open-endedness. Where the creation accounts underwrite ideas of completeness and a fixed form for human being, evolutionary theory posits fitness and adaptation. Too often, in popular imagination, the conceptualization of evolution drifts toward teleology, as if there is a single trajectory of development along which humans progress. Evolution is often used as a near synonym for this notion of progress toward a predefined goal. In contrast, genetic studies have clarified that even genes themselves are often more like concentrations of potentials than rigid templates. For example, all locusts are also grasshoppers; they are just grasshoppers whose aggressive swarming potentials have been activated by environmental conditions.

Teleology, with its sense of "oughtness," does not effectively describe human nature. What humanity will be is not yet known and can be known only in the becoming. At what point in the process of evolution might we say that the *imago Dei* was attained, or sufficiently represented to be recognizable as such? And given that evolution is not a singular trajectory, is it possible that humanity might lose the divine image? One alternative to this line of thinking is that the openness to development and change is what makes us image bearers. Our cognition is composed in part of the whole history of our species' interaction with the world, along with the capacity to respond to what is new. This line of reflection raises the thorny notion of divine contingency or God's becoming. Indeed, divine becoming remains a significant challenge for Christian theology; *imago Dei* is one of a number of doctrines that touch on that pressure point.

The final disruption pertains more to evolutionary theory than to theology. Competition and survival remain the primary paradigms in evolutionary theory, but those terms tend to mask aspects of the process of evolution. In my estimation, what most distinctively characterizes the interplay between systems is responsiveness, rather than competition. Attention to cognitive psychologies shifts the focus to relatedness, interaction, adjustment, and the exercise of wisdom as we face ever-changing contexts. We have evolved cognitively to be well suited to adjust and interact. The three Types of thinking allow for maximum responsiveness to established patterns (Type 1), to new or especially complex information (Type 2), and to widespread conflicts in systems, whether individual or collective (Type 3).

Responsiveness, interrelatedness, and wisdom in choosing among options are all themes of theological interest. The dominant presentation of theories of evolution has tended to overlook or even conceal such factors. But our minds are the result of that very sort of responsiveness and openness to all the rest of reality. Theology promotes this sort of unified sense of the material world and, in this case, offers a corrective to the atomized paradigm that typifies evolutionary theory.

Conclusion

This essay has considered a constructive (as opposed to apologetic function) for *imago Dei*, through a process akin to reverse engineering. Rather than relegating it to a more poetic role, nudging theological anthropology in the direction of human dignity or perhaps destabilizing dominant identities, I have explored how a rigorous consideration of human mentalizing might illuminate something of the divine whose image we bear. The realities of human cognition suggest several correctives to our theology of God and theological anthropology. Attention to cognitive psychology, its evolution and its function in religious cultures, integrates relationality, contextuality, and materiality in ways that the reason-transcendence paradigm of *imago Dei* does not. It also captures claims about the nature of God that remain subsidiary in other theological constructs, such as attention to relationality as constitutive of human and divine being, rather than merely a capacity that we can exercise. These tentative observations warrant reflection that pushes both more deeply and expansively. It is the sort of theological reflection that the rare interdisciplinary hospitality and academic community of CTI helps to facilitate.

4

Nicholas of Cusa's Mystical Theology in Theological and Scientific Perspective

Textuality, Intersubjectivity, Transformation

ANDREA HOLLINGSWORTH

Fifteenth-century Cardinal, reformer, and mystic Nicholas of Cusa is well known for his innovative mystical ideas and practices, which he related to new ways of understanding God and the church. Among his most important mystical texts is *De visione Dei* or *De icona* (hereafter *De visione*),[1] a prayerful and poetic mid-career work that is probably the best-known and most frequently studied of Nicholas's writings. My intention in this essay is to interpret *De visione* with an eye to its experiential "texture"[2] (especially its affective contouring), and proceed to analyze that texture with a view to contemporary psychology and neuroscience. In so doing, I hope

1. References to Nicholas of Cusa's works are based on the Heidelberg Academy edition: *Nicolai de Cusa Opera Omnia* (Hamburg: Felix Meiner). English translations of *De docta ignorantia* and *De visione Dei* are from H. Lawrence Bond, *Nicholas of Cusa: Selected Spiritual Writings* (New York and Mahwah, NJ: Paulist Press, 1997).

2. In Cognitive Poetics—a field lying at the intersection of literary linguistics and cognitive psychology—scholars often speak of the "texture" of a literary work. To say that a text has texture is to say that what a text *means* is intricately tied to what it *does* in the mind of a reader. See Peter Stockwell, *Cognitive Poetics: An Introduction* (London and New York: Routledge, 2002).

to make a case that the treatise's phenomenological contouring is such that it has the ability to orchestrate a process of embodied, experiential transformation-of-self in the reader.

I begin with a historical and thematic introduction to Nicholas's *De visione*, and a sketch of key methodological presuppositions that underlie my approach to the text. I then offer an original interdisciplinary interpretation of the treatise. My reading is based on Boston University neuroscientist Patrick McNamara's theory of the transformation of the self in religious experience. It engages, as well, select developmental and clinical psychological researches on relationality and emotion regulation. My aim is to trace ways in which the embodied, relational, prayerful journey represented in this work may indeed have elicited profound, salutary transformation in the selves of readers by way of experience-dependent neuroplastic processes.[3] This journey, as I shall explain, consists of four "moments": *Decentering, Rupture-Repair, Reappraisal*, and *Integration*. In theological terms, the *telos* of this four-moment path is deification, Christification, or union with God. In psychological terms, it is a more integrated, emotionally regulated identity. Either way, what emerges is a self[4] with strengthened volitional power, which

3. A growing body of neuroscientific evidence suggests that contemplative practices have potential to alter the functional and structural plasticity of neural processes that mediate emotion regulation, attention, and empathy. See, e.g., Gaëlle Desbordes, Lobsang T. Negi, Thaddeus W. W. Pace, B. Alan Wallace, Charles L. Raison, and Eric L. Schwartz, "Effects of Mindful-Attention and Compassion Meditation Training on Amygdala Response to Emotional Stimuli in an Ordinary, Non-Meditative State," *Frontiers in Human Neuroscience* 6 (November 1, 2012); Britta K. Hölzel, James Carmody, Mark Vangel, Christina Congleton, Sita M. Yerramsetti, Tim Gard, and Sara W. Lazar, "Mindfulness Practice Leads to Increases in Regional Brain Gray Matter Density," *Psychiatry Research: Neuroimaging* 191, no. 1 (January 30, 2011): 36–43; Sara Van Leeuwen, Wolf Singer, and Lucia Melloni, "Meditation Increases the Depth of Information Processing and Improves the Allocation of Attention in Space," *Frontiers in Human Neuroscience* 6 (2012): 133; Glen L. Xiong and Murali Doraiswamy, "Does Meditation Enhance Cognition and Brain Plasticity?" *Annals of the New York Academy of Sciences* 1172 (2009): 63–69.

4. There is of course no Latin equivalent to the English word "self," which first appeared in the poetic and theatrical works of seventeenth-century writers like John

manifests as a deepened capacity to *choose* the way of self-control
and kindness over that of pettiness, selfishness, and cruelty.[5] This
interdisciplinary interpretation of *De visione* offers a new window
onto Nicholas's understanding of God as a dynamic, transforming
reality into which the mind of his reader-contemplator is progres-
sively ushered.

Introducing *De visione Dei*

De visione was written in 1453 for a group of spiritually zealous Bene-
dictine monks with whom Nicholas was closely acquainted.[6] The
brothers of St. Quirin monastery in Tegernsee wished for Nicholas to
weigh in on some debated questions concerning mystical theology's
essential nature and means of realization.[7] So Nicholas sent them a

---

Donne and William Shakespeare. Knowing full well the difficulties that plague the
word "self"—especially when we are talking about a premodern thinker like Nicholas, for whom notions of "selfhood" and "subjectivity" as commonly understood
today would be quite foreign—I nevertheless still choose to utilize this term. I think
"self" can function as a helpfully vague umbrella category under which Nicholas's
various iterations of first-person human experience may find a place.

5. Patrick McNamara, *The Neuroscience of Religious Experience* (Cambridge:
Cambridge University Press, 2009), xii.

6. Four hundred and fifty-four of the letters between Nicholas and the brothers
at the monastery in Tegernsee have been preserved in Munich's *Staatsbibliothek*. Of
these, only a handful have been edited and released. Thirty-six appear in Edmond
Vansteenberghe, "La correspondence de Nicolas de Cuse avec Gaspard Aindorffer
et Bernarde de Waging," in *Autour de la docte ignorance: Une controverse sur la
théologie mystique au XVe siècle*, Beiträge zur Geschichte der Philosophie des Mit-
telalters (Münster: Aschendorff, 1915), xiv. Some of the letters have been translated
from Latin into French and German and published. Thomas Izbicki has translated
the letters in Vansteenberghe into English, but his work remains unpublished. I am
grateful to Tom for sharing his translations with me.

7. The monks were especially keen for Nicholas to address the so-called *intel-
lectus-affectus* controversy, which involved disagreement over whether knowledge,
or love, or both together (and in what order) most define the essence of mysticism
in the Dionysian tradition. For a detailed treatment of this debate (and Nicholas's
role in it) see K. M. Ziebart, *Nicolaus Cusanus on Faith and the Intellect: A Case*

text designed to serve as a mystical guidebook. Nicholas's stated aim is to "lead you experientially into the most sacred darkness" in such a way that "each of you, in the measure granted him by God, will of himself endeavor to draw continuously nearer [to the inaccessible light]."[8] Thus *De visione* is rooted in its ability to coax forth in the reader a contemplative experience of edging ever closer to the dark brilliance of the divine. As H. Lawrence Bond says, *De visione* "is crafted to 'picture' by its own rhetorical form and with a variety of linguistic devices so as not merely to 'signify' but, in the manner of icons, to transpose the reader . . . from one contemplative state to another."[9]

In the preface, the monks are instructed to participate in a unique exercise (a "paraliturgy," as Bernard McGinn[10] describes it) involving coordinated procession before an "all-seeing" icon—a painting depicting a face whose eyes seem to rest on the viewer from whatever angle the image is observed. In *De visione*'s early and middle chapters, we find extended meditations on the opposite yet coinciding relationship between (on one hand) the limited perspective of finite creatures, and (on the other hand) the all-encompassing perspective of the Infinite God, whose providential, life-giving face and gaze "never abandons anyone."[11] The latter chapters of the work underscore the doctrines of the Trinity and Christ's Incarnation, and emphasize divine love along with *theōsis* (divinization).

An important unifying thread in the treatise is, of course, *visio Dei*, the vision of God. This refers both to the mystery of God's

---

Study in Fifteenth-Century Fides-Ratio Controversy, Studies in Intellectual History Series 225 (Leiden: Brill, 2014).

8. *De visione* prologue, #1.11–14 (h VI, 4).

9. H. Lawrence Bond, "The 'Icon' and the 'Iconic Text' in Nicholas of Cusa's *De Visione Dei* I–XVII," in *Nicholas of Cusa and His Age: Intellect and Spirituality*, ed. Thomas M. Izbicki and Christopher M. Bellitto (Leiden: Brill, 2002), 183.

10. Bernard McGinn, "Seeing and Not Seeing: Nicholas of Cusa's *De Visione Dei* in the History of Western Mysticism," in *Cusanus: The Legacy of Learned Ignorance*, ed. Peter J. Casarella (Washington, DC: Catholic University of America Press, 2006), 39.

11. *De visione* V, #15.6 (h VI, 18).

gaze, which, though unlimited and ungraspable, is nevertheless the creative ground of all things, *and* to the mystery of the human gaze, which, though finite or "contracted," comes to share in divine sight when turned toward the infinite loving Face in and by which it is continually brought into being. In God's infinite vision is enfolded a coincidence of subject and object such that God's gaze turns out to be the deep meaning of the self's own act of gazing upon God.[12] In *De visione*, gazing and being-gazed-upon become a sort of "possibility space" in which the contemplator is guided to enter more and more into his best potential mode of existing.[13]

Methodological Considerations

The analysis below is based on the thought that, by attending to various textual elements in *De visione* (e.g., words, speech forms, images, ideational features), and by tracing the ebbs and flows of such elements across the text's chapters and paragraphs, it becomes possible to gain a sense of the cognitive and affective texture of Nicholas's treatise—its broad, temporally conditioned phenomenological topography. Especially relevant is the ebb and flow of positively and negatively valenced features. For example, we can track the salience and nonsalience of, on one hand, love (*caritas, amor*)—which Nicholas, along with much of the Christian tradition, associates with affinitive, compassionate tending or minding of the other—and, on the other hand, awe or holy fear (*admiratio*)— which Nicholas associates with the unpleasantness of hunger, the encounter with the monstrous, and the pain of self-violence.[14] It

---

12. Werner Beierwaltes, "*Visio facialis—Sehen ins Angesicht. Zur Coincidenz des endlichen und unendlichen Blicks bei Cusanus,*" *Mitteilungen und Forschungen der Cusanus-Gesellschaft* 18 (1989): 91–124, 100.

13. *De visione* IV, #9.16–19 (h VI, 14).

14. *De docta ignorantia* (*DDI*) prologue 1–5 (h I, 1–2); *De visione* IX, #37.5–7 (h VI, 34–35).

then becomes possible to compare the waxing, waning, and weaving of differently valenced textual features to the flow of mental states that empirical psychological sciences suggest tend to mark transformation-of-self toward conditions of greater socioemotional health. To the degree that *De visione*'s experiential patterning mirrors that of healthy human self-development and therapeutic change, we can begin to see ways in which an implied reader's contemplative encounter with Nicholas's treatise might tap and rehearse psychobiological processes that can heal and form human minds toward more integrated and regulated ways of being in the world.

I assume that mystical theology is a practice. As scholars like Charles M. Stang, Barbara Newman, and Sara Poor have shown,[15] the study of mystical theological texts cannot be divorced from the study of the performative acts of reading, writing, and copying—things that were, in medieval times, considered to be deeply spiritual. As such, analysis demands expansion beyond the narrow view of the "inner experience" of a single historical author. That mystical theology is a practice means it may be analyzed with a general practitioner in mind, as is sometimes done in ritual studies. The subjectivity of this practitioner can be called the "implied reader" or "implied contemplator." In our case, this would be a monk at St. Quirin monastery who was already familiar with common formal and ideational elements of medieval Christian mystical theological reflection, who knew main tenets of Nicholas's thought, and who was eager to embark on the spiritual journey set out by the text.

The Transformation of the Contemplative Self in Four Stages

Having briefly considered some key historical, theological, and methodological issues, we are now ready to delve into the heart

15. See their essays in *The Cambridge Companion to Christian Mysticism*, ed. Amy Hollywood and Patricia Z. Beckman (Cambridge: Cambridge University Press, 2012).

of this essay's constructive argument. Patrick McNamara has recently offered a promising theory about neurocognitive processes that underlie religious experiences and practices and their self-transforming effects. I think McNamara's theory, utilized with some amendments and supplementations, can shed light on how Nicholas of Cusa's mystical theological writings may indeed have served to guide implied readers into their ownmost possibilities for integrated, virtuous living.[16]

McNamara's model is rooted in what he identifies as a significant anatomical overlap between brain areas involved in religious experience and those involved in self-consciousness. McNamara argues that transformation in a religious context begins when the individual's self-concept or self-structure is "decentered," that is, temporarily decoupled from its control over executive cognitive functions. A search then commences, through semantic memory, for an ideal self that more closely matches the individual's needs, goals, and values. Often, in religious contexts, this ideal self corresponds with an ancestor, saint, or god. Finally, with the help of grammars that carry meaning and value, the old self is joined to the new self and there emerges a larger, more complex, more unified identity.[17] Neurobiologically, what results is an increase in neural integration—which is to say, greater functional connectivity between brain areas responsible for automatic perception and those responsible for conceptualization, valuation, and planning. The entire process, in McNamara's summation, "reduces to an attempt to shed an old [s]elf and attach to and become a new higher [s]elf."[18]

In what follows, I build on McNamara's neurocognitive model

16. Elsewhere, I have discussed the strengths and limitations of McNamara's theory as compared to other scientific models of religious experience. See Andrea Hollingsworth, "The Architecture of Apophasis: Exploring Options for a Cognitive Scientific Interpretation of the Via Negativa," *Religion, Brain and Behavior* 6, no. 4 (2016): 290–306.

17. McNamara, *The Neuroscience of Religious Experience*, 46–47.

18. McNamara, *The Neuroscience of Religious Experience*, 54.

of religious experience to suggest that Nicholas's *De visione* leads its implied reader-contemplator through a similar four-stage journey of transformation-of-self. Before I unpack this claim, a brief description of the preface's paraliturgical ritual with the all-seeing icon is in order.[19] After introductory greetings, Nicholas instructs the monks to hang the all-seeing painting (which he had sent to Tegernsee with the treatise) on a wall. They are to, first, arrange themselves equidistantly before it (in a semi-circle), and look at it. In doing so, each brother will "experience that from whatever place one observes it the face will appear to regard him alone," and will be "astonished" (*admiratio*) when he considers that the gaze "looks on all and each one . . . at the same time." Next, the brothers are told to fix their eyes on the gaze while walking from west to east, and then back again from east to west, in opposite directions. Each will thus "discover that the icon's gaze continuously follows him" at all times. Finally, each brother is instructed to "ask the other [brother]" whether he too experienced the gaze following him during the procession in opposite directions. When his query is met with "yes," the brother will "believe" his comrade even though it does not seem possible. In believing, he will discover that "the face looks unfailingly on all who walk before it even from opposite directions."[20]

1. Decentering

Decentering, on McNamara's model, is an event in which the "executive [s]elf" is temporarily "taken off-line" from its control over the attentional and behavioral goals of the individual. The transient relaxing of cognitive control that decentering effects is a quieting of what McNamara also calls, following Thomas Aquinas, the "agent intellect."[21]

19. Here I follow the three-phase description set forth by Michel de Certeau in "The Gaze: Nicholas of Cusa," *Diacritics* 17, no. 3 (Autumn 1987): 2–38.

20. *De visione* preface (h VI, 5–7).

21. McNamara, *The Neuroscience of Religious Experience*, 39–41.

At the heart of Nicholas's extraordinary opening ritual, there is, I submit, a profound destabilization-of-self that serves to launch a process of change, of deepened and expanded selfhood, in the implied contemplator. In Michel de Certeau's words, the exercise "dislodge[s] [Nicholas's] addressees from their prejudicial position," and thus "'mak[es] way' for the Cusan theory" of the Infinite God beyond the wall of the *coincidentia oppositorum*.[22] The gaze is eminently uncanny and beyond all objectification. Both everywhere and nowhere, it is immanent to all but identical to none. New points of view (and thus, new meanings) are spawned and juxtaposed with each passing second, each step taken, each astonished interchange.[23] For the implied contemplator, this results in a deepened awareness of the limited, perspective-bound status of human being and knowing, as well as an oblique intuition of the absolute center and circumference of all perspectives, which remains infinitely beyond all human grasping.[24] As K. M. Ziebart puts it, it is precisely in its status as a disturbing "affront to reason" that the all-seeing icon is, for Nicholas, "an effective tool in the practice of mystical theology."[25] It is no accident that *admiratio*—which, as previously noted, carries a dysphoric, provocative affective connotation in Nicholas's thought—is thrice mentioned in *De visione*'s preface.

Though confrontation plays an important role in *De visione*'s preface, affinitive affectivity is crucial as well. Each brother is explicitly urged to meditate on "how this gaze deserts no one" and how it "takes diligent care of each."[26] Later in the treatise, Nicholas indicates that the infinite gaze of God, which "never

---

22. *De visione* XI–XIII (h VI, 39–49).

23. De Certeau, "The Gaze: Nicholas of Cusa," 16–17.

24. "He will marvel at how its gaze was moved, although it remains motionless, and his imagination will not be able to grasp how it is moved in the same manner with someone coming forth to meet him from the opposite direction." *De visione* preface, #3.16–18 (h VI, 6).

25. Ziebart, *Nicolaus Cusanus on Faith and the Intellect*, 193.

26. *De visione* preface, #4.5–7 (h VI, 6).

abandons,"[27] looks on all and each for the purpose of bringing each one into its best possible state of being.[28] We are here dealing, I suggest, with something like what developmental psychologist Vasudevi Reddy calls the "gaze at grips with me," by which is meant the infant's feeling of being lovingly faced and attended to. Reddy's empirical and theoretical work suggests that the experience of this feeling in infancy gives rise to cognitive structures that support attention (and the higher-level cognitive and socioemotional abilities attention makes possible) later in life.[29] Thus, while it is true that the opening-to-the-other in the initial moments of mystical reflection in Nicholas's thought unseats the autonomous agential self, it is also the case that this uncomfortable disorientation is a relational *re*orientation. As we shall see, this dance between disestablishment and reestablishment takes on a complex and neuropsychologically significant patterning as the treatise further unfolds.

2. Rupture-Repair

The second step in McNamara's model is transitional. It consists of the launch of an "offline"[30] search through semantic memory to identify an "ideal [s]elf" that more closely matches the aims and values of the individual. In this phase, the agentive self is placed in a "suppositional space" that holds a "stock of existing identities stored in semantic memory."[31] In keeping with this model, the section of Nicholas's *De visione* that follows immediately upon the preface

27. *De visione* V, #15.6 (h VI, 18).

28. *De visione* IV, #9.16–19 (h VI, 14). Cf. *DDI* I, 1.1–2 (h I, 5).

29. Vasudevi Reddy, "On Being an Object of Attention: Implications for Self-Other Consciousness," *Trends in Cognitive Sciences* 7, no. 9 (September 2003): 397–402; Vasudevi Reddy, *How Infants Know Minds* (Cambridge, MA: Harvard University Press, 2008).

30. "Offline," in McNamara's usage, means decoupled from working memory.

31. McNamara, *The Neuroscience of Religious Experience*, 50.

(chapters I–VIII) facilitates the implied contemplator's entrance into a kind of suppositional space.

First, there is a clear inward turn at the beginning of chapter IV. Here the treatise shifts dramatically from a third-person propaedeutic voice to a second-person prayerful voice, spoken on behalf of (or in place of) the reader. After being instructed once again to perform a communal procession in front of the omnivoyant painting, the monks are told: "[A] contemplation will arise in you, and you will be stirred saying: 'Lord, in this image of you I now behold your providence by a certain sensible experience.'"[32] The reader's attention is thus directed suddenly and intensely to his own inwardly voiced prayer. Inward attention and internal dialogue are markedly evident elsewhere in this section. For example, in chapter VII, we read: "And when I thus rest in the silence of contemplation, you, Lord, answer me within my own heart, saying: 'Be yours and I too will be yours!'"[33]

However, there is an even more striking sense in which this portion of the text witnesses to the contemplator's process of being shepherded into a space of new possibilities. Certain of De visione's textual features and their temporal patterning function, I suggest, in such a way as to generate a complex sequence of emotional responses in readers—a sequence that is healingly self-formative. The text's potential to orchestrate this emotional cadence is made possible in large part by the valenced nature, the positive or negative affective tonality, of particular textual elements. Some text features are likely to be appraised by the reader as, for example, conducive to goal achievement, familiar and expected, undemanding on coping resources, and intrinsically pleasurable. The ideational feature of *divine providence*, which is generally linked to God's presence, guidance, benevolence, and trustworthiness (and, in De visione, to God's loving face and gaze), is likely to activate precisely this sort of

32. *De visione* IV, #9.6–8 (h VI, 13).
33. *De visione* VII, #25.12–14 (h VI, 26–27).

appraisal pattern, and thus to give rise to positive emotion. Other features are apt to be appraised in a different manner—that is, as obstructive to goal achievement, unfamiliar and/or unpredictable, taxing on coping resources, and intrinsically unpleasant. Nicholas associates his famed doctrine of *learned ignorance* (and the *admiratio* implied in it)[34] with the discomfort of hunger, the encounter with the monstrous, and the pain of self-violence,[35] all of which suggests that this ideational feature carries a negative emotional valence in his writings, and would be prone to influence the implied reader accordingly.[36]

Now if we proceed to trace and compare the prominence or salience of providence and ignorance in the first third or so of the treatise, an interesting pattern emerges. The two features are, as it turns out, significantly negatively correlated (−.61, to be precise). Figure 1 charts this oscillatory relationship. In the graph, the X-axis represents paragraphs in *De visione* as they progress sequentially, and the Y-axis represents degree of salience/prominence.[37]

When providence rises in salience—for example: "You do not forsake me, Lord; you guard me on every side, for you take most diligent care of me"[38]—then the salience of ignorance tends to drop. Conversely, when ignorance rises in salience—for instance: "This

34. For Nicholas, "learned ignorance" is the idea that God or the Infinite is utterly incomprehensible and hidden, and cannot be known except through a leap past all images, analogies, and determinate knowledge. This theme is suffused throughout his writings, and is pronounced in *De visione*.

35. *DDI* prologue 1–5 (h I, 1–2); *De visione* IX, #37.5–7 (h VI, 34–35).

36. It is also of course the case that for Nicholas, *docta ignorantia* is the doorway to the ultimate goal of mystical theology, that is, knowledge of and union with God. The value of *ignorantia* in Nicholas's thought consists precisely in its status as a painful epistemic and spiritual obstacle; in unseating *ratio*, it prepares the way for the illumination of *intellectus*. K. M. Ziebart's reading of Nicholas's mystical thought brings out the negativity of *ignorantia* quite lucidly. See Ziebart, *Nicolaus Cusanus on Faith and the Intellect*.

37. Dr. Kenneth Reynhout deserves enthusiastic thanks for his assistance with quantitative textual analysis, as displayed in figures 1, 2, and 3.

38. *De visione* IV, #10.7–8 (h VI, 14).

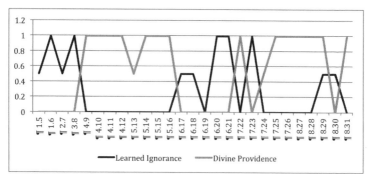

Figure 1

cloud, mist, darkness or ignorance into which whoever seeks your face enters when one leaps beyond every knowledge and concept is such that below it your face cannot be found except veiled"[39]—then the salience of providence tends to fall.

How, from a scientific perspective, might such an oscillating rhythm be said to open new possibilities for selfhood? My thought is that it parallels, and evokes in the implied reader, affective and interpersonal "rupture-repair" rhythms that serve to facilitate neural integration and foster self-regulation in individuals. The picture painted by theorists in developmental neurobiology and clinical psychology is that rupture-repair dynamics play a crucial role in the emergence of healthy, well-regulated personalities, and in the healing of fractured selves.[40] Neurobiologically, such emergence is theorized to coincide with increased neural integration. Thus, many contemporary relational and attachment therapies with adults are designed to facilitate biopsychosocial healing and growth by, in

39. *De visione* VI, #21.4–7 (h VI, 23).

40. See, for example, Jeremy D. Safran and Jessica Kraus, "Alliance Ruptures, Impasses, and Enactments: A Relational Perspective," *Psychotherapy, Therapeutic Relationship* 51, no. 3 (2014): 381–87; Jeremy D. Safran, J. Christopher Muran, and Catherine Eubanks-Carter, "Repairing Alliance Ruptures," *Psychotherapy, Evidence-Based Psychotherapy Relationships* 48, no. 1 (2011): 80–87; Mario Mikulincer and Phillip R. Shaver, *Attachment in Adulthood: Structure, Dynamics, and Change* (New York: Guilford, 2007), 75–76.

some sense, rehearsing the socioemotional rhythms of rupture and repair discussed above, thereby enhancing the client's capacity for self-regulation and empathy. I think the cadences of Nicholas's mystical theology in the first third of *De visione*—the recurring vacillations between *ignorantia* and *providentia*—operate in an analogous way. The contemplator is guided, via a rupture-repair rhythm, into a "possibility space" (McNamara)—or, in the theological symbolism of *De visione* IV, an expansion of the self's capacity to receive the grace that enables one to embody Christic virtue.[41]

3. Reappraisal

In McNamara's third stage there occurs a search through semantic memory for the "ideal [s]elf" in whom the conflicted parts of the psyche can be unified. Narrative grammars that hold rich symbolic meaning help along the search process, the ultimate goal of which is a "link-up" between the old self and the new, ideal self. "If this link-up succeeds," McNamara writes, "it can bring to the personality a new level of integration, a reduction in internal conflict, and a new access to internal cognitive, emotional, and behavioral resources that were unthinkable for the old [s]elf."[42] As in stage two, defining phenomenological features of stage three include inwardly directed attention, internal dialogue, and altered awareness or perception.[43]

My suggestion is that the middle third of *De visione* (chapters IX–XVI) shepherds the implied reader through an inward search not unlike what McNamara describes, and further, that this search transpires by means of cognitive reappraisal strategies. A crucial element of self-regulation and a frequent goal of psychotherapeutic treatment, cognitive reappraisal is the practice of shifting inward meanings, especially those that carry potential to mire a person in

---

41. *De visione* IV, #11.1–12 (h VI, 15).
42. McNamara, *The Neuroscience of Religious Experience*, 53.
43. McNamara, *The Neuroscience of Religious Experience*, 151.

anxiety, depression, and other negative emotional states. Cognitive reappraisal involves slowly and deliberately training the mind to consider a disturbing thought or circumstance—for instance, a fearful feeling of uncertainty—from new angles so that multiple ways of reorienting oneself in relation to negativity become possible. Neurologically, cognitive reappraisal corresponds with modulations in the amygdala (a brain structure that plays a large role in the fear response) as well as prefrontal control systems.[44]

Consistent with both McNamara's stage three "search" and cognitive reappraisal strategies, what we see happening in *De visione* IX–XVI is a quest to come to a new appraisal of self, the infinite divine other, and the relation between them. In this quest, the contemplator is guided to not only tolerate, but to reinterpret positively (and with existential relevance) the incomprehensibility and inaccessibility of the Absolute.

The main motif in this part of the text is divine infinity,[45] and Nicholas's famed doctrine of the *coincidentia oppositorum*—which is pictured as a "wall" to the paradise where God dwells—is presented as the "way in" to the vision of the Infinite. For Nicholas, the coincidence of opposites is "simplicity where contradictories correspond."[46] Of the thirty-six total appearances of the term *coincidentia/coincidere* in *De visione*, a striking twenty-eight (78 percent) are found in these middle chapters. This means that the implied contemplator's experience at this point in the meditative/readerly

---

44. For an overview of neural bases of self-regulation, especially cognitive reappraisal processes, see Kateri McRae, Kevin N. Ochsner, and James J. Gross, "The Reason in Passion: A Social Cognitive Neuroscience Approach to Emotion Regulation," in *Handbook of Self-Regulation: Research, Theory, and Applications*, 2nd ed., ed. Kathleen D. Vohs and Roy F. Baumeister (New York: Guilford, 2011), 186–203.

45. And actually, as Werner Beierwaltes has demonstrated, a strong case can be made that the idea of infinity lies at the crux of Nicholas's mystical theology on the whole. Werner Beierwaltes, "Mystische Elemente im Denken des Cusanus," in *Deutsche Mystik im Abendländischen Zusammenhang* (Tübingen: Max Niemeyer Verlag, 2000), 425–48.

46. *DDI* III, Epistola, #264.14–16 (h I, 163).

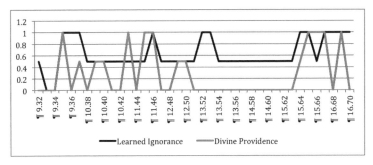

Figure 2

journey involves practicing what it means to hold together, and come to a qualitatively new understanding of, fundamentally contrasting meanings.

I think Nicholas's *coincidentia oppositorum* is as much a means for retraining the mind and emotions in ways that heal and integrate the self as it is a tool for approaching metaphysical and theological puzzles with creativity and nuance. One way this becomes evident is when we observe the relationship between oppositely valenced text features in this section. Let us again take providence and ignorance as indicative.

In Figure 2, we see that the negative correlation (the rupture-repair rhythm) of the previous section has, in this text portion, disappeared. Where providence and ignorance before displayed a strongly significant –.61 correlational value, exhibited by the mirrored zigzags of the dark and light lines in Figure 1, they now show an insignificant .16 value, evinced by the general absence in Figure 2 of this crisscross pattern. So, whereas at the beginning of the treatise these two oppositely valenced elements exhibited a relationship of juxtaposition and oscillation, in the middle portion of the treatise they are, comparatively speaking, more entwined or co-occurring. This attests, I think, to the reader's journey of coming to reappraise the negativity of divine unknowability. The painful feeling of alienation resulting from keen awareness of God's radical transcendence and the limitations of human finitude is slowly *folded into* a larger sense of attuned trust in God's immanence and loving care, *despite* unceasing ambiguity and unknowing. This intense "coincidenting" of (on one hand) positive emotions linked to the idea of divine presence, and (on the other hand) negative emotions tied to the idea of divine inaccessibility, bears kinship with McNamara's search for an ideal self. It amounts to a search for a new appraisal scheme or semantic construct of the relation between oneself and the divine other—a way of coming somehow to love, trust, and feel the "presence" of abyssal Infinity, even though this Infinity is beyond all objectification and human grasp.

4. Integration

The last stage in McNamara's theory consists of a "binding" or integration of the old self with the ideal self that slowly surfaced in the search through semantic memory in stage three. The result of this "link-up" is a new identity that is larger, more complex, more unified, and more emotionally and behaviorally regulated.[47] Increased integration of neural structures and systems, along with increased self-regulatory abilities, means expanded possibilities for moral actions like curbing impulses, responding flexibly in thorny social situations, and acting with compassion toward others.[48] Phenomenological features of this fourth stage include positive affect, insight, and meaningfulness.[49]

Above I argued that, in Nicholas of Cusa's *De visione*, the equivalent of McNamara's stage three search is the quest for a self in whom the opposites of God's radical transcendence and unknowability, and God's radical immanence and providential love, are folded into a new appraisal scheme or meaning construct. I now

47. McNamara, *The Neuroscience of Religious Experience*, 46–47.
48. McNamara, *The Neuroscience of Religious Experience*, xii.
49. McNamara, *The Neuroscience of Religious Experience*, 151.

want to suggest that the final section of *De visione* (chapters XVII–XXV) is aimed at realizing the reader's process of becoming unified with this new self who lies beyond the *coincidentia oppositorum*. For Nicholas, Jesus Christ is the ultimate One in whom opposites coincide, and it is he who is now explicitly identified as the divine exemplar with and in whom a new identity is sought. I suggest that the McNamaran "binding" stage—which in theological terms is called *theōsis*,[50] *filiatio*, or *Christiformitas*—comes about in this final section through the tapping and strengthening of socioemotional cognitive processes dedicated to *simulation* (that is, interpersonal mirroring or resonance systems).

As McNamara's model predicts increased positive emotion in this final stage, I want to begin by pointing out the conspicuous affective shift in the last section of the treatise. With some exceptions, the overall focus in *De visione* XVII–XXV moves away from cognitively destabilizing language and content, toward an emphasis on the trinitarian and incarnate love of God.[51] In fact, I have tracked a 40 percent decrease in apophatic language use (which I take to be negatively valenced), and a corresponding 41 percent increase in positively valenced text features, in the final nine chapters of the treatise as compared to the previous sixteen.[52] There is thus

50. For a detailed treatment of the doctrine of *theōsis* in Nicholas's thought, see Nancy J. Hudson, *Becoming God: The Doctrine of Theosis in Nicholas of Cusa* (Washington, DC: Catholic University of America Press, 2007).

51. As Clyde Lee Miller says: "Nicholas begins to stress the affective side of both God's attracting and human responding. . . . Heartfelt warmth and affection pervade Nicholas' prayerful teaching as he reflects on the mysteries of faith." Clyde Lee Miller, "Nicholas of Cusa's *The Vision of God*," in *An Introduction to the Medieval Mystics of Europe*, ed. Paul Szarmach (Albany: State University of New York Press, 1984), 293–312.

52. There is an upsurge in text elements such as: a warm, relational linguistic tonality; the ideational motif of divine love; affirmations of a sense of being watched (benevolently gazed upon); affirmations of a sense of encountering divine responsiveness; and affirmations of a feeling of "sweetness." At the same time, there is a corresponding drop in the frequency of features like: aphaeresis (abstraction); double proposition semantics; split, fused, and shifting reference; the juxtaposition

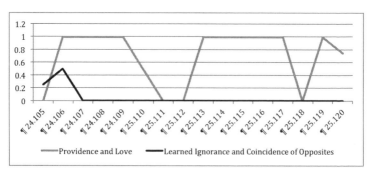

Figure 3

a return to the negative correlation between oppositely valenced elements that was first observed in the early part of the treatise. But now, instead of oscillating, the salience of positive features generally remains high, while that of negative features generally remains low. This dynamic is particularly striking in the treatise's final two chapters, as Figure 3 demonstrates. As the text draws to a close, themes of providence and love predominate, while the coincidence of opposites and learned ignorance fade into the background.

In accordance with this positively valenced affective turn, I believe textual evidence supports the thought that simulative or imitative neurocognitive systems based largely in the brain's reward system underlie the implied reader's self-transforming "binding" to the ideal—to Christ, the eternal exemplar—in these closing chapters. Much cognitive and neuroscientific evidence suggests that humans process social information by means of simulation; that is, we understand the movements, intentions, and emotions of others with reference to our own movements, intentions, and emotions. This "mirror" or "resonance" circuitry appears to be distributed throughout frontal, parietal, and temporal lobes; is closely linked to the brain's reward system; and is thought to underlie human interper-

of personal and impersonal symbols of God; and subject-predicate fusion. For a detailed treatment of such apophatic linguistic devices, see Michael A. Sells, *Mystical Languages of Unsaying* (Chicago: University of Chicago Press, 1994).

sonal understanding.[53] Moreover, many developmental neuropsychologists believe that mirroring behaviors in infancy (between a child and primary caregiver) are crucial in human attachment and self-development, and support capacities for emotion regulation and moral agency in later life.[54]

As Hoff has observed, Nicholas of Cusa places a distinct emphasis on the *imitatio Christi* in his spirituality and theology.[55] We see a clear example of this emphasis in *De visione* XXII.97, where the contemplator is led to meditate upon the relation of similitude between Christ's way of perceiving, and ours. Especially highlighted is Christ's way of gazing with compassionate understanding into the faces and eyes of human others:

> For while you walked in this world of sense, you, Jesus, used eyes of flesh similar to ours. . . . And . . . according to the forms of the face and of the eyes of the people whom you saw, you were the true judge of the soul's passions, of its anger, joy, and sorrow. And more subtly still, from a few signs you comprehended what lay

53. For a relatively up-to-date treatment of the mirror system, see chapter 8 of Michael Gazzaniga, Richard Ivry, and George Mangun, *Cognitive Neuroscience: The Biology of Mind* (New York: W. W. Norton, 2013). On the role of imitation in infant development, see Andrew Meltzoff, "Social Cognition and the Origins of Imitation, Empathy, and Theory of Mind," in *Handbook of Childhood Cognitive Development*, 2nd ed., ed. Usha Goswami (Oxford: Blackwell, 2011), 49–75.

54. See, for example: Allan Schore, *Affect Dysregulation and Disorders of the Self* (New York: W. W. Norton, 2003); Allan Schore, *Affect Regulation and the Repair of the Self* (New York: W. W. Norton, 2003); Louis Cozolino, *The Neuroscience of Human Relationships* (New York: W. W. Norton, 2014); Daniel Siegel, *The Developing Mind* (New York: Guilford, 2015).

55. Johannes Hoff, *The Analogical Turn: Rethinking Modernity with Nicholas of Cusa* (Grand Rapids: Eerdmans, 2013), 214. To imitate Christ (or to become *Christiformitas*) is, for Nicholas, to enter into a relation of "disproportional likeness" to the infinite (*De Possest* #10.15 (h XI, 12). It is also to come into the deepest truth and highest potential of oneself. For Nicholas, Christ is not an extrinsic exemplar to any human person; rather, because in the incarnation he is united to human nature, Christ is the most ultimate (and the most immediate) truth of each person's existence (cf. *De venatione sapientiae* I, #3 [h XII, 5–6]).

hidden in the mind of a human being. For nothing is conceived in the mind that is not in some way signaled in the face, most greatly in the eyes, because the face is the heart's messenger.[56]

Here the implied reader is guided to envision, in marvelous detail, Jesus's affectively attuned encounters with people.[57] As subsequent chapters make clear, the subtext here is injunctive—something akin to: Imitate Christ's *way of seeing*; allow it to be a seed in your own heart which grows, through the *potentia* of the Spirit, into the fruits of the Spirit.[58]

Might this sort of imaginative imitation of a religious exemplar hold potential to spur the emergence of a stronger and more morally capable agentive self, as McNamara's model would predict? Neuroscientist Michael L. Spezio would likely answer in the affirmative. In a recent article, Spezio argues that virtue formation in religious contexts crucially involves simulative socioemotional cognition.[59] For a religious exercitant to imitate or simulate an exemplar's acts of love is for said exercitant to follow after the *way in which* the exemplar matches his emotion and action to fit the unique personhood, dignity, and needs of the other.[60]

This is just the kind of imitation that, I suggest, is encouraged

---

56. *De visione* XXII, #94.6–7, 12–17 (h VI, 74–75).

57. It is important to note that this passage is wrapped up in a broader theological-metaphysical reflection on the nature of the hypostatic union. However, when we view it in terms of the treatise's overall status as a practical guidebook to a self-transforming vision of God through filiative conformity to Christ, the passage is cast in a new light.

58. In *De visione* XXIV–XXV (h VI, 82–90), Jesus is seen to be the Word of Life planted in the soil of the human heart, and the Spirit is figured as the potency or power that actualizes the gradual growth and perfection of this seed.

59. Michael L. Spezio, "Social Neuroscience and Theistic Evolution: Intersubjectivity, Love, and the Social Sphere," *Zygon: Journal of Religion and Science* 48, no. 2 (2013): 428–38.

60. Spezio, "Social Neuroscience and Theistic Evolution," 433–34; See also Linda Zagzebski, *Divine Motivation Theory* (Cambridge: Cambridge University Press, 2004), 102.

in the self of the implied reader at the close of *De visione*. Nicholas's mystical masterpiece is contoured in such a way as to guide the reader through a meditative journey that culminates in precisely this experience of intimacy by way of filiative conformity to Christ the eternal exemplar. The aimed-for result is a stronger, more integrated self—a self with a deepened capacity or foundation of possibility for actualizing Christic qualities like goodness, justice, and attentive, merciful love for others.[61]

Existing in the "Best Manner Possible"

In a recent article, Norwegian theologian Knut Alfsvåg states that the "basic idea" of Nicholas's *De visione* is that "human beings realize themselves in the gaze of God."[62] Such self-realization, he suggests, occurs through the exercise and strengthening of free will, which in turn coincides with "grow[th] in conformity to the divine foundation of one's existence."[63] I am in basic agreement with Alfsvåg's claim that the relationally mediated development of the self—specifically, the growth of the self's capacity to freely will in conformity with Christ the Exemplar—is at the heart of *De visione*'s theological message. However, based on my preceding analysis, I would go further than he.

Specifically, I would submit that the text does not merely *describe to* the reader, but also carries potential to *call forth in* the reader, in a radically embodied way, the sort of growth to which Alfsvåg refers. I wish to be very clear that I am *not* proposing that Nicholas somehow "knew about" neuropsychological "mechanisms" of human growth and change. Rather, my ultimate suggestion is that

61. *De visione* IV, #11.1–15 (h VI, 15–16).
62. Knut Alfsvåg, "*Explicatio* and *Complicatio*: On the Understanding of the Relationship between God and the World in the Work of Nicholas Cusanus," *International Journal of Systematic Theology* 14, no. 3 (July 2012): 295–309, 302.
63. Alfsvåg, "*Explicatio* and *Complicatio*," 302.

our assessment of Nicholas's theological legacy—especially with respect to the Christian mystical theological tradition—ought to include recognition of and appreciation for the striking ways in which his spiritual writings tap into embodied and socially conditioned dynamics that contemporary psychological sciences view as important for the development and healing of human selves.

5

Religious Persecution and Religious Freedom

....

The Witness of Russia's New Martyrs and Holy Elders

JOHN P. BURGESS

Interdisciplinary conversation encourages a scholar to ask questions—and explore answers—that might otherwise not suggest themselves. As a Christian theologian who has recently spent a year at the Center of Theological Inquiry talking to legal scholars, I have found myself asking new questions about a legally guaranteed right to religious freedom. What in the Christian tradition works for or against establishing such a right? When would such a right appear to be a necessary expression of Christian love and regard for others? And when might such a right appear to threaten social, historical norms that the Christian religion has helped shape and that the church wishes to preserve?[1]

My commitment to thinking in the spaces between different worlds of discourse goes beyond the question of scholarly disciplines. I am a North American who has spent more than a decade following social and political developments in post-communist

1. The contributions of the Christian tradition to Western notions of religious freedom have been thoroughly documented in the work of John Witte Jr. See, for example, his book *Christianity and Human Rights* (New York: Cambridge University Press, 2010).

Russia. And I am a Protestant theologian deeply shaped by the great figures of the Reformation, especially John Calvin and his successors, who is also intensely interested in the Eastern Orthodox tradition, especially as it developed among the eastern Slavic peoples in Russia, Ukraine, and Belarus. A theologian among legal experts, an American-born US citizen among Russians, and a Protestant among Orthodox believers—in each case, my travels into "foreign lands" have not only broadened my intellectual horizons but also reshaped my scholarly work, making it more attentive not only to the cross-fertilization but also to the tensions that inevitably arise between different angles of vision.[2]

My constant moving back and forth between contrasting scholarly, cultural, and theological worlds has provoked the question that I investigate in this essay: How should a Christian theologian understand the implications of religious persecution for religious freedom? I am referring specifically to the massive persecution that religious communities in Russia, and especially the Russian Orthodox Church, suffered under communism in the twentieth century. I believe that theological reflection on the experience of religious persecution has important lessons for Christians today—Orthodox, Catholic, and Protestant alike—about a legally guaranteed right to religious freedom.

My concern is, above all, theological. Other scholars have helpfully reviewed and analyzed the constitutional and legal status of religious freedom today in the Russian Federation as well as the official positions of the Russian Orthodox Church on human rights and religious tolerance.[3] In addition, Western observers are carefully

2. See my book *Encounters with Orthodoxy: How Protestant Churches Can Reform Themselves Again* (Louisville: Westminster John Knox, 2013).

3. See T. Jeremy Gunn, "The Law of the Russian Federation and the Freedom of Conscience and Religious Associations from a Human Rights Perspective," in *Proselytism and Orthodoxy in Russia*, ed. John Witte Jr. and Michael Bourdeaux (Maryknoll, NY: Orbis, 1999), 239–64; Christopher Marsh, *Religion and the State in Russia and China* (New York: Continuum, 2011), 123–29; and Kristina Stoeckl, *The Russian Orthodox Church and Human Rights* (New York: Routledge, 2014).

documenting incidents of religious intolerance that occur in Russia today, and investigating the ways in which a resurgent Orthodox Church has sought a religious monopoly in its society.[4] As valuable as these perspectives are, my interests go in a different direction.

Since the fall of communism, the Russian Orthodox Church has canonized more than two thousand of its adherents who, it judges, remained true to their faith as they suffered because of it, sometimes unto death, under the Bolshevik regime. I believe that the church's cult of the twentieth-century "new martyrs" suggests an understanding of religious freedom that implicitly commits Christians to a legal right to religious freedom. What made the new martyrs remarkable was not that they suffered—millions of Russians were victims of Bolshevik repression—but rather how they suffered. In the church's view, they responded to persecution neither passively nor violently, but rather by asserting Christian freedom. They refused to let their persecutors define them as enemies of the state, and they refused to see their oppressors simply as enemies. Christian freedom meant the freedom both to refute communist ideology and to regard the agents of this ideology as human beings claimed first of all by God, not the state and its demands for conformity.

The Cult of the New Martyrs

In referring to a "cult" of the new martyrs, I mean not a rigid religious sect, but rather a set of religious practices and rituals that honor persons whom a religious community has deemed to be holy. Among Christians, it has been especially Catholic and Orthodox churches that have cultivated cults of the saints, including veneration of their pictorial representations (such as icons) and their

4. Especially important is the work of Forum 18. See http://www.forum18.org/. See also Geraldine Fagan, *Believing in Russia: Religious Policy after Communism* (New York: Routledge, 2013).

physical remains (relics). The church sets aside days in its calendar (typically the anniversary of the saint's death) to honor them and provides for composition of life histories, hymns, prayers, and worship services in their memory. While the saints inspire by their earthly example, they are also believed to be living presences to whom believers turn in prayer for support and guidance.

Catholic and Orthodox churches have developed formal procedures of canonization. In contemporary Russian Orthodoxy, a patriarchal commission on canonization receives nominations, conducts investigations, and makes recommendations to the Patriarch and a synod of bishops. Every time that the church approves a canonization, it lifts up spiritual and moral values that it believes represent the highest ideals of the Christian life in the church's contemporary social context. At times in the past, the church has primarily venerated princes and warriors who defended the nation and its religious heritage, reminding believers of their duty to the motherland. At other times, the church has venerated great monks or nuns, thereby calling believers to attend to prayer and ascetic discipline. Since the fall of communism, it has been especially the cult of the new martyrs that has shaped the identity of the Russian Orthodox Church.

The degree of persecution that the Russian church suffered is unfamiliar to most North Americans and in any case unfathomable to Russians and Americans alike today.[5] From the outset, eradication of religion was central to the Bolshevik program. Persecution of the church began within days after the October Revolution. Priests were arrested and killed; parishes were robbed of precious

5. For good histories of the Russian Orthodox Church under communism, see Hans-Christian Diedrich, *"Wohin sollen wir gehen . . .": Der Weg der Christen durch die sowjetische Religionsverfolgung* (Erlangen: Martin-Luther Verlag, 2007); Nathaniel Davis, *A Long Walk to Church: A Contemporary History of Russian Orthodoxy* (Boulder, CO: Westview, 2003); Dimitry Pospielovsky, *The Russian Church under the Soviet Regime, 1917–1982*, 2 vols. (Crestwood, NY: St. Vladimir's Seminary Press, 1984); and Christopher Marsh, *Religion and the State in Russia and China* (New York: Continuum, 2011).

icons and liturgical implements; and churches, monasteries, and religious schools were closed. By 1940, at the conclusion of Stalin's Great Terror, fewer than three hundred parishes, out of more than fifty thousand in 1917, remained open. As many as 90 percent of clerics and monastics had been arrested; most would be executed or perish under the harsh conditions of the Gulag. Scholars estimate that 200,000 persons or more died for their faith. The Russian Orthodox Church as a public institution was reduced to a few smoldering embers. What remained of church life largely went underground.

Hitler's invasion of the Soviet Union in 1941 forced Stalin to alter course. To win popular support in the areas that they conquered, the Germans allowed churches and monasteries to reopen. Stalin responded in kind, seeking to win popular support against the Nazis. By the end of the war, as many as fifteen thousand parishes and one hundred monasteries were again operating. But new waves of persecution broke out in the 1950s under Khrushchev, and although few believers were executed for their faith, the state intensified its efforts to educate the population in Marxist-Leninist principles of scientific atheism. By the 1980s, the church had been reduced to seven thousand parishes and eighteen monasteries. State authorities with the help of the KGB vetted seminarians, controlled appointment of priests and bishops, and forbade the church from conducting social work or lay religious education.

With the rise of Gorbachev and his policies of *glasnost* and *perestroika*, the church won space for public witness. In 1988, the state allowed the church to celebrate the millennium of Christianity in Rus'. In 1989, the church canonized Tikhon (Belavin), who had been elected Patriarch in 1917 and had valiantly defended church interests until his death in 1925. In 1991, the dissolution of the Soviet Union completely freed the church from state control. Today, more than 33,000 parishes and eight hundred monasteries are active, the church operates an extensive network of social ministries, and as many as 80 percent of Russians identify as Orthodox. Church leaders speak of the "rebirth" of Orthodox Christianity; two American scholars have coined the term "Orthodoxy resurgent."[6]

The new freedom of the church in society has been accompanied by interest within the church in those believers who preserved the Christian faith during the harshest years of Soviet repression. Today, some church leaders even assert that the martyrs of the 1920s and 1930s sowed the seeds of faith that have now sprouted into new religious life.[7] The "spiritual freedom" of the martyrs laid the foundation for the "social freedom" of the church in the new Russia.

Of special significance in raising the profile of the new martyrs was a Jubilee Bishops Council in 2000. After participating in the reconsecration of Moscow's Christ the Savior Cathedral, which in 1931 had been razed at Stalin's orders, Patriarch Aleksii II and the bishops received an icon of the *sobor* (assembly) of the new martyrs and confessors "both known and unknown" and glorified approximately one thousand of them. Since then, another one thousand new martyrs have been canonized, increasing the total number of historic Russian saints by five times. Nearly every parish and monastery has now identified its new martyrs, and their names dominate the church's calendar and prayers. The new martyrs represent not only famous personalities, as in the canonizations of earlier periods, but also ordinary priests, monks, nuns, and lay men and women who heroically witnessed to their faith.

The cult of the new martyrs actually includes three major groupings of saints. The first consists of martyrs in the strictest sense of the word: people who were executed for their faith. A second group is composed of "confessors," people who suffered for their faith—often experiencing the harrowing conditions of the

6. See John Garrard and Carol Garrard, *Russian Orthodoxy Resurgent: Faith and Power in the New Russia* (Princeton: Princeton University Press, 2008).

7. Church leaders often cite the famous words of the ancient Christian theologian Tertullian: "The blood of the martyrs is the seed of the Church." See, for example, the website of the Parish of the Cathedral of the New Martyrs of Podol'skii: http://neomartyrs.ru/index.php/novomucheniki/podvig-muchenichestva.

prison camps—but managed to survive. The members of the third group are known as "passion-bearers," those who did not suffer directly for their faith but nevertheless endured persecution and execution in a Christian spirit.

The fact that in the eleventh century Russia's first canonized saints, Boris and Gleb, were passion-bearers opened the way for including the royal family, the Romanovs, in the *sobor* of 2000, a matter that had generated considerable controversy both in the canonization committee and in the Russian Orthodox Church more widely. The church today regards Czar Nicholas II as a pious but highly flawed political leader who died not because he professed the Orthodox faith but because the Bolsheviks wished to destroy all traces of the old social and political order. The church nevertheless venerates him, his wife Alexandra, and their children Olga, Maria, Anastasia, Tatiana, and Aleksei on account of the extraordinary Christian equanimity and love that they reportedly demonstrated after their arrest and imprisonment and as they faced their executors on July 17, 1918.

The Character of Spiritual Freedom

The presence of inner, spiritual freedom is a key criterion that the canonization commission applies when nominating persons who fit in any of these three categories. In the church's view, the new martyrs (and confessors and passion-bearers) demonstrated the freedom, as the apostle Paul expressed it, to speak "the truth in love" (Eph. 4:15). The new martyrs retained their dignity before God by keeping a clear conscience and speaking the truth to their enemies, while striving to show their enemies that persecuted and persecutors alike were beloved children of God.

The church contrasts this way of inner, spiritual freedom with alternative strategies during the Soviet era. Some believers chose the way of political dissidence, either wanting the church to be a free space in which they could gather and support each other or agitating for the church hierarchy to denounce the Bolsheviks or even to work to overthrow them. A second response to the new political order was political opportunism. The so-called "Renovationists" supported the new communist regime. They hoped that Bolshevik persecution of the official church would allow them to seize control of the church and realize ambitious reforms, such as celebrating the liturgy in the vernacular rather than Church Slavonic, allowing for married bishops, and replacing the Patriarchate with democratic church government.

A third approach came to characterize the official church after Patriarch Tikhon died and Metropolitan Sergii (Stragorodskii) assumed his powers. In 1927, Sergii issued a declaration of loyalty that would become infamous in its apparent willingness to have the church compromise with the new Soviet government. Sergii sought to preserve the church as a public, legal institution by allowing the state to control it. The church could continue to celebrate the liturgy in a limited number of parishes but only at the price of publicly declaring its full support of Soviet policies.

Today, the church has judged that all three of these alternative strategies fell short. Each compromised the church's freedom. The dissidents confused Christian freedom with political freedom. They failed to see that Christians can be free under any political order and that, indeed, Christian freedom allows believers to rise above political divisions and machinations. The Renovationists also succumbed to the temptation of political power. Rather than consulting the wisdom of the church as a whole—through the scriptures, the church's ancient traditions, and church councils—they sought to impose reform from above and in dependence on the coercive power of the state. The result was ecclesiastical schism. And Metropolitan Sergii mistakenly believed that the church could trade away its inner, spiritual freedom for institutional security. History demonstrated that the state took advantage of Sergii's compliance not to preserve but rather to destroy the church.

The new martyrs aimed not at institutional church power, but rather at enabling believers to live freely before God and with their fellow human beings. This kind of inner, spiritual freedom has deep roots in the Christian scriptures and church tradition. Christ refused to present himself as a political leader (John 18:36–38). He foreswore both political revolution and political compromise. His aim was not to guarantee or reform the life of a religious institution, but rather to gather believers into a living community of worship, mutual care, and loving service. Similarly, the apostle Paul thinks of himself as free because he is able to proclaim the gospel regardless of external circumstances. Even imprisonment does not abridge this freedom (Acts 28:30–31).

The Russian Orthodox tradition has often understood this Christian freedom to be exemplified especially well by the lives of "holy elders" (*startsy*).[8] During the Soviet period, at a time in which the church hierarchy was deeply compromised by cooperation with the state, the holy elders represented a spiritual authority that did not depend on institutional or political power. Their wisdom seemed to come directly from God. Their deep dedication to prayer and ascetic discipline helped them discern God's will and resist pressures to conform to worldly powers.

Many of these holy elders suffered harassment, arrest, and imprisonment, only to emerge stronger in faith. Pilgrims, sometimes by the thousands, traveled to remote parts of Russia to visit them, ask their counsel, and receive their blessing. The holy elders radiated an unconditional love that at the same time moved people to see the truth about their sinful lives and their need to repent. While few have been canonized—their ability to challenge not only political but also church authority complicates their status in the eyes of the canonization commission—they continue to enjoy considerable popular veneration. People flock to their gravesites, display and revere their photographs, and pray to them for assistance.

8. See Irina Paert, *Spiritual Elders* (DeKalb: Northern Illinois University Press, 2010).

JOHN P. BURGESS

Some of the tradition's holy elders have been "fools for Christ," seemingly mentally disturbed people who nevertheless spoke truth to power, like the fool in Shakespeare's *King Lear*. In the Soviet period, Archimandrite Pavel (Gruzdev) sometimes liked to play this role. As one of his disciples has written, "holy fooling" enabled Pavel to express his opposition to prevailing political structures, even as it protected him from them. The authorities did not know what to do with an apparent madman and mostly left him alone after arresting and interrogating him.[9]

Other holy elders became renowned for faithfully maintaining the church's cycles of prayer and worship, even after the authorities forbade them from serving and closed their churches or monasteries. In 1941, Archimandrite Seraphim (Tiapochkin) was arrested for secretly celebrating the liturgy at the factory to which he had been assigned after his parish was closed. Sentenced to ten years in a labor camp, there too he secretly celebrated the liturgy and gave spiritual counsel to fellow believers. As his term drew to an end, the prison commander summoned him and asked what he intended to do upon release. When Seraphim replied, "I am a priest, I will serve [the liturgy]," the commander said, "Well, if you are going to do that, then I am going to give you five more years in prison."[10]

The holy elders were also known for keeping confidences. People felt safe in revealing to them whatever was on their hearts. Whenever a holy elder spoke aloud about his or her spiritual children, he or she never put their spiritual or physical well-being at stake, a matter of special importance during the Soviet era. When the secret police arrested the holy elder Pavel (Troitskii), he acknowledged violating Soviet law but refused to implicate anyone

9. See Viktor Mamontov, "Rodnik Liubvi [Wellspring of Love]," *Christianos* 16 (2007); http://krotov.info/history/20/1990/mamontov.htm.

10. See Viktor Mamontov, "Serdtse pustyni: Zhizneopisanie arkhimandrita Serafima (Tiapochkina) [The Heart of the Desert: The Life of Archimandrite Serafim (Tiapochkin)]," *Pravoslavnaia Obshchina* 49; http://pravoslavni.ucoz.ru/news/arkhim_viktor_mamontov_serdce_pustyni/2011-06-01-464.

else: "I conducted illegal worship services solely out of personal disagreement with the laws of the Soviet regime. . . . My religious convictions prohibit me from naming others who were involved."[11]

What is evident from all of these examples is that the holy elders always treated others, including the Bolsheviks themselves, with love and consideration, never with hatred or disdain. Even the holy fool sought to humanize his interrogators, to make them laugh at themselves. The holy elders spoke the truth in a way that did not drive their opponents into a defensive posture but rather respected them. The new martyrs took a similar path. They too sought to combine truth-telling and loving service, formation of eucharistic community among believers with concern for those outside the church. Worship and prayer kept the new martyrs rooted in an inner, spiritual freedom that radiated joy and confidence in God's provision even in the face of death. They renounced political power, but their freedom for God and other human beings had political implications: all humans should have the social freedom to hear the church's invitation to freedom in the gospel.

Handling Interrogation

The Bolshevik persecution of believers was wicked not only in its magnitude but also in its strategy. The state sought to deny their victims the status of martyrdom. The martyrs of the early church had clearly died for their faith. They had refused to worship the civic gods and had rejected acts of sacrilege against the God of Jesus Christ. The Bolsheviks, in contrast, did not persecute Christians for refusing to subscribe to their "gods" (Marxist ideology or atheism), but rather accused them of participating in "counter-revolutionary"

11. See "*Novomucheniki i Ispovedniki Russkoi Pravoslavnoi Tserkvi 20 veka: Pavel (Troitskii Petr Vasil'evich)*; http://kuz3.pstbi.ccas.ru/bin/nkws .exe/koi/nm/?HYZ9EJxGH0xITYZCF2JMTcCid74gdS1We5slCHYlTcGZeu -yPq7m9X2pTX0yTaxWQWslBE*.

activities. Christians were supposed to confess that they sought to overthrow the new government and restore the Czar.

Speaking the truth in love was especially put to the test when believers faced arrest and interrogation. Sometimes they were subjected to mental or even physical torture. Other times they were tempted to agree with their interrogators' accusations in a misguided effort to establish trustworthiness and personal connection. The church's commission on canonization does not condemn those who broke down. But only a person who refused to betray him- or herself or others can be glorified as a saint. Typical is the church's account of Father Ioann (Vasil'ev), who was arrested in 1936 for continuing to serve as a priest, even though state authorities were closing parishes. Interrogators did not ask him to confess to being a practicing priest but rather taunted him for being a political traitor: "You conducted counter-revolutionary activities, didn't you? Do you confess your guilt?" When Father Ioann simply replied, "No, I do not," he was condemned to death for lying, ostensibly about his politics, not his faith.[12]

To the church, telling the truth in love in these circumstances meant openly acknowledging, in accordance with Romans 13, that all government has been established by God. In the church's view, the new martyrs did not challenge the authority of the Bolshevik state. The secret police protocol of March 22, 1938, included in a church biography of the new martyr nun Maria (Tseitlin), is representative:

Q: What are your convictions and views about the Soviet government?

A: As a believer, I understand every government to be from God,

12. See Igumen Damaskin (Orlevskii), "Sviashchennomuchenik Nikolai (Tochtuev) [Holy-Martyr Nikolai (Tochtuev)]," in *Zhitia Novomuchenikov i Ispovednikov Rossiiskikh 20 veka: Mai [The Lives of the New Russian Martyrs and Confessors of the 20th Century: May]* (Tver': Bulat, 2007), 33.

102

and it does not concern me who has power at the present moment in the Soviet Union.[13]

Orthodox believers affirmed that despite evils of the new regime, it had come to power only because God had so ordained. At the same time, they did not hesitate to confront the authorities with their crimes, especially against the church, just as Paul and the apostles had openly criticized the Jewish authorities for persecuting them and their followers (Acts 25:10–21). Maria's protocol continues:

Q: As a monastic have you been subject to repression from the side of the Soviet government?
A: As a monastic I have been deprived of a right to vote.

Q: You were arrested for counter-revolutionary activities that you undertook with other nuns of the Novodevichii Monastery. The interrogation requires a truthful response.
A: I went into an apartment with the nuns Evdokia (Golovanova) and Matrona (Lipatova). I said that a difficult time has arrived . . . [and] believers are discontent with the Soviet government. . . . The Soviet government is robbing monasteries [and] closing churches, but soon they will pay with their lives [and] everyone will then know that there is a God.[14]

We see here that inner, spiritual freedom meant, above all, freedom from fear. One no longer feared what the Bolsheviks could do to one's body (Matt. 10:28). And spiritual freedom also meant freedom to respect the Bolshevik persecutors as people. The new martyrs,

13. See "Prepodobnomuchenitsa Mariia (Tseitlin) [The Nun-Martyr Maria (Tseitlin)]," in *Novomucheniki moskovskogo Novodevich'ego Monastyria [The New Martyrs of Moscow's Novodevichii Monastery]* (Moscow: Novodevichii Monastery, 2006), 24.
14. "Prepodobnomuchenitsa Mariia (Tseitlin)," 24.

like the holy elders, refused to dehumanize those whom they saw to be evil.

In the context of Soviet persecution, humanizing the enemy meant rejecting violent resistance against him. Traditionally, the Russian Orthodox Church has canonized warriors who fought with arms to save the nation from foreign invaders, such as Alexander Nevskii (thirteenth century, Swedes) and Dmitrii Donskoi (fourteenth century, Tartars). The new martyrs, however, saw Bolsheviks not as foreigners, but rather as brothers and sisters who in many cases had been baptized into the Orthodox Church and had attended its schools or seminaries, as had Lenin and Stalin. In the view of the canonization commission, the new martyrs displayed holiness in their commitment to calling the Bolsheviks back to their true identity as Russians shaped by an Orthodox culture and its moral values.

Russian church historian Aleksandr Mazyrin has recently written of the spiritual achievement of the Holy-Martyr Bishop Petr (Polianskii), who served as Patriarchal Representative after Patriarch Tikhon's death. Soon after assuming office, he was arrested and exiled to northern Siberia. Petr suffered from debilitating health problems, including a serious heart problem. Over the next decade, he regularly appealed to Evgenii Tuchkov, head of the Bolshevik secret police, for mercy, even while refusing to submit to Tuchkov's demands that he first renounce his position of church authority.[15]

I ask you to consider my point of view—and then you will be persuaded that I am right and cannot act otherwise [in church affairs]. If you open your eyes, you will see that there is no reason to think badly of me, and all the less reason to apply such cruel measures. . . . Forgive me that I write so frankly—I am lan-

15. Aleksandr Mazyrin, *Kifa: patriarshii mestobliustitel' sviashchennomuchenik Petr, Mitropolit Krutitskii (1861–1937) [Cephas: Holy Martyr Peter, 1861–1937, Metropolitan of Krutitskii, as the Patriarchal Representative]* (Moscow: St. Tikhon's University Press, 2012), 714.

guishing physically and need your help. . . . I earnestly ask you to lighten my suffering.[16]

As another church historian, Vladimir Vorob'ev, has written: "[Under the circumstances of Bolshevik persecution, it was necessary] to 'give no excuse to those seeking one.' Only one path remained . . . to try to find in one's enemy, even an enemy of the church, some dimension of humanity and to appeal to this humanity in the hope that he would suddenly be moved . . . and ashamed . . . and choose mercy. This strategy required meekness and humility."[17] The new martyrs sustained a remarkable sense of the dignity that God had given both them and others, including the Bolsheviks.

The Lessons of Persecution

A liberally minded Westerner could suppose that the experience of persecution would be enough to convince any religious group that it should exercise religious toleration and support a legally guaranteed right to religious freedom. This logic has historical evidence to support it. In his magisterial review of the history of Christian social thought, German theologian Ernst Troeltsch (1865–1923) argued that persecuted and socially marginalized Christian minorities, such as the Anabaptists and Baptists, helped impel the political arguments in the West for separation of church and state and protection of freedom of conscience.[18] More recently—and in reference to Russia—church historian Hans-Christian Diedrich has written

16. Mazyrin, *Kifa*, 831–32.

17. Vladimir Vorob'ev, "Predislovie [Foreword]," in *Kifa: patriarshii mestobliu-stitel' sviashchennomuchenik Petr, Mitropolit Krutitskii (1861–1937) [Cephas: Holy Martyr Peter, 1861–1937, Metropolitan of Krutitskii, as the Patriarchal Representative]* (Moscow: St. Tikhon's University Press, 2012), 8.

18. Ernst Troeltsch, *The Social Teaching of the Christian Churches*, trans. Olive Wyon (Louisville: Westminster John Knox, 1992).

eloquently that because all the churches suffered persecution under communism and offered up martyrs, all are called today to "grieve, remember, and pray together. For the dead no longer know any confessions, dogmas, traditions, or divisions. They are encircled by the great bond of the unity and the peace of those who stand before God."[19]

Nevertheless, history demonstrates that the experience of religious persecution can have the opposite effect on a religious community. As historians Elizabeth Castelli and Candida Moss have noted, religious groups that have experienced martyrdom often claim a privileged status in society.[20] The experience of martyrdom offers them a sense of spiritual purity and superiority over others. Too often, yesterday's persecuted become tomorrow's persecutors. Having suffered in the past, a group attacks its present-day opponents or competitors as dangerous and even demonic. Some political observers fear that just such a process is taking place today in the Russian Orthodox Church, despite its immense suffering under communism. Rather than committing itself to religious freedom, the church is seeking to establish itself as a privileged cultural and social force.

The ability of the cult of the new martyrs to underwrite liberal-democratic notions of a right to religious freedom is further complicated by lack of historical evidence that the new martyrs themselves ever called on the Bolshevik state to respect other religious groups. The new martyrs were focused on their own spiritual integrity, not on questions of religious toleration or legally guaranteed religious rights. In most cases, we simply do not know what they thought about Jews, Muslims, or minority Protestant and Catholic groups in Russia that also suffered persecution—although

19. Diedrich, "*Wohin sollen wir gehen*," 429.
20. Elizabeth Castelli, *Martyrdom and Memory* (New York: Columbia University Press, 2004), 196; Candida Moss, *Ancient Christian Martyrdom* (New Haven: Yale University Press, 2012), 17; and Candida Moss, *The Myth of Persecution* (New York: HarperOne, 2013), 247–60.

we do have the example of a renowned holy elder of the Soviet period, Tavrion (Batozskii), who embraced his Lutheran and Catholic neighbors as brothers and sisters in Christ.[21]

I am less interested, however, in the historical and sociological aspects of what persecuted groups do when the persecution ends, than in the vision of life before God to which the Russian Orthodox Church points with the help of the cult of the new martyrs. Regardless of the Orthodox Church's relations with other religious groups in Russia, its cult of the new martyrs offers unique theological resources for thinking about Christian freedom—and a right to religious freedom in society—today.

Russian Orthodox Church historians who have studied the new martyrs judge them to have been apolitical or to have claimed a space "above politics."[22] The new martyrs did not organize a political party or movement, but rather took the course of Patriarch Tikhon, who refused to align the church either with the Bolsheviks or the Whites, those Russians who remained loyal to the Czar and fought with arms against the new regime until their defeat in the early 1920s. The new martyrs, like the holy elders, insisted that Christians be lovingly present to all members of society, regardless of their political loyalties. The inner, spiritual freedom of the new martyrs expressed itself not as a program for reforming political structures, but rather as a way of relating lovingly to persecutors.

This "human factor," as historian Vorob'ev calls it, was the only viable option for Christians in a time in which "rule by law" was absent.[23] What made the new martyrs remarkable was their ability to preserve their personal dignity, while insisting on the dignity

---

21. See Viktor Mamontov, "Otets pustyni: Zhizneopisanie startsa Tavriona (Batozskogo) [The Father of the Desert: The Life of Holy Elder Tavrion (Batozskii)," *Pravoslavnaia Obshchina* 26: 83–91; https://elitsy.ru/profile/18050/153486/.

22. See Alexander Mazyrin, *Vyshie ierarkhi o preemstve vlasti v Russkoi Pravoslavnoi Tserkvi [Highest Church Hierarchs on the Question of Conferring of Power in the Russian Orthodox Church]* (Moscow: St. Tikhon's University Press, 2006), 397.

23. Personal conversation, July 19, 2015.

of those who sought to rob them of dignity—and therefore only robbed themselves of dignity. This dignity was more than a general humanistic concept; it was a God-given dignity, whose contours had been revealed most fully in the life and death of Jesus Christ. The new martyrs saw themselves participating in Christ's self-giving love, which included confessing loyalty to God above all earthly powers. As Kirill, the current Russian Patriarch, has argued, the church learned in the Soviet era that political dissidence led only to social marginalization. Christians had to "speak with the surrounding world [knowing that in this dialogue] *the one who is internally stronger triumphs.*"[24]

The new martyrs declared that true freedom comes not from the state, but from God. Spiritually free people are loyal to God above any other social or political force. They will not be surprised if the state resents their freedom to resist its ideologies as well as its demands for unquestioned allegiance. The spiritually free person can therefore expect criticism and opposition—and even oppression and persecution.[25] In the Russian Orthodox tradition—and arguably in the Christian religion more generally—believers should willingly accept such suffering. "Suffering in freedom" tests and purifies Christian freedom, allowing believers to make a public witness to their reliance on God alone (1 Peter 2:18–24).

Inner, spiritual freedom never remains simply "inner and spiritual," however, if we mean "passive and antisocial." The inner, spiritual freedom of the new martyrs, while "apolitical" or "above politics," nevertheless has political implications, if we understand politics to be more than a competition for domination, but rather

24. See Sophia Kishkovsky, "Russian Orthodox Church Elects Outspoken Patriarch," *New York Times*, 27 Jan. 2009; http://www.nytimes.com/2009/01/28/world/europe/28orthodox.html?_r=1&.

25. The twentieth-century Protestant theologian Karl Barth develops similar themes in his political writings. See, for example, his *Against the Stream: Shorter Post-War Writings, 1946-52*, ed. Ronald Gregor Smith (New York: Philosophical Library, 1954).

the way in which people organize their life together in society, as the introductory essay to this volume makes clear.

The Russian Orthodox Church's experience of religious persecution in the twentieth century underwrites an ethic of speaking the truth in love. This ethic displays the humanity both of Christ and of those who have supremely exemplified his way: the holy elders, the saints, and the martyrs. If this ethic applied to the way in which Christians treated their Soviet enemies and persecutors, it surely applies all the more to the circumstances of pluralistic societies in which Christians constantly interact with people who do not persecute them yet assert beliefs and values that contradict those of the church.

Where rule by law is possible—as it is in most Western societies today—those who are spiritually free, it seems to me, should promote a legally guaranteed right to freedom of religion for at least two reasons. First, the spiritually free church will not want to draw others into its life solely on the basis of social custom or privilege. A faith that is coerced, whether explicitly or implicitly, is no faith at all.[26] A genuine faith endows freedom—freedom for God, freedom for others, and freedom to speak the truth in love. Second, the spiritually free church seeks a protected social space in which it can invite others to know this freedom in Christ. A legally guaranteed right to religious freedom gives the church room to invite people into the freedom of the gospel.[27]

Paradoxically, "spiritual freedom" seeks "religious freedom" yet does not depend on it. A spiritually free church seeks a legal right to conduct its activities and a legal right for individuals to respond to the church's invitation to be free. If the state, however, opposes the church, the church will be ready to stand alone, even to go

---

26. See Aristotle Papanikolaou, *The Mystical as Political* (Notre Dame: Notre Dame University Press, 2012), 1–12.

27. The Russian Orthodox Church has developed these themes in its *Social Concept* (2000). For an analysis, see Irina Papkova, *The Orthodox Church and Russian Politics* (New York: Oxford University Press, 2011), 22–32.

underground, in the confidence that God will ultimately vindicate it. Again, spiritual freedom is ultimately a matter of the church's faithfulness to God, not a matter of what the state does.

Spiritual Freedom versus Religious Freedom

To be sure, spiritual freedom and religious freedom do not always complement each other in everyday social life. A society characterized by a right to religious freedom often appears to reduce freedom to a matter of personal "consumer" choice. The Russian Orthodox Church often expresses concern that instead of guaranteeing a social space in which people are able to discover spiritual freedom, "religious freedom" becomes an ideology of individualistic self-determination that demands ultimate allegiance and therefore is demonic. The church regularly expresses its uneasiness about a "Western" moral relativism that appears to threaten rather than preserve the church's free space.[28]

Nevertheless, the cult of the new martyrs declares that Christians best respond to social opposition and competition not by asking the state to secure legal privileges for the church, but rather by cultivating an inner, spiritual freedom to speak the truth in love. Believers will see their opponents and competitors as children of God and therefore as brothers and sisters with whom they share responsibility for a just, peaceable social order. Those who are spiritually free will declare that they are ultimately *for* others, not against them. The church will call its opponents and competitors back to what it regards to be their true selves: people created to know God and to live in the same spiritual freedom that believers seek for themselves.

The Russian Orthodox Church does not always seem to have learned these lessons. Perhaps no religious community ever does.

28. Papanikolaou, *Mystical as Political*, 43–54.

The Christian quest for freedom, like all theological ventures, demands humility and hope, as the introductory essay to this volume so powerfully demonstrates. Humility, because inner, spiritual freedom always remains elusive and a right to religious freedom is always under negotiation in society. Hope, because despite Christians' failings and missteps, the Truth whom Christians worship has promised them nothing less than to set them—and the whole creation—free (John 8:32; Rom. 8:21). The new martyrs lived with this humility and hope, as do those of us who, though not persecuted for faith, move back and forth between profoundly different and sometimes contradictory academic disciplines, national cultures, and religious traditions.

6

Law, Theology, and Aesthetics

....

Identifying the Sources of Authority

MARY ELLEN O'CONNELL

Since at least the seventeenth century, certain Western philosophers, legal scholars, politicians, and even theologians have worked
to keep religion separated from law and legal institutions.[1] The separation has been attempted for wholly understandable reasons. An
early impetus was the fact that Christians in Europe were developing conflicting theologies that could not support a common law.
At least in theory, the separation of law and religion was largely
completed by the mid-twentieth century and is now generally taken
for granted.[2] Few scholars advocate a return to the Middle Ages.

---

1. The theologian and legal scholar Hugo Grotius is often credited with beginning this development when he said: "What we have been saying [about law] would
have a degree of validity even if we should concede that which cannot be conceded
without the utmost wickedness, that there is no God, or that the affairs of men are
of no concern to him." See Hugo Grotius, *Law of War and Peace*, Prolegomena,
para. 11 (1625). See also Brad Gregory, who describes Grotius's predecessor as well
as successor theologians who influenced the quest to separate law and public life
from religion in Brad S. Gregory, *The Unintended Reformation: How a Religious
Revolution Secularized Society* (Cambridge, MA: Harvard University Press, 2012).

2. For interesting discussions of the impossibility of truly separating law and
religion, see, e.g., Samuel Moyn, *Christian Human Rights* (Philadelphia: University

112

Yet, the separation of law and religion has had certain significant negative unintended consequences for law. Among these negative consequences is the loss of an explanation for the concept of legal authority. In the West, religious ideas once provided such an explanation, as religion still does in large parts of the Muslim world, in Israel, and other communities.[3] In place of religion, legal scholars attempted to use science as a substitute, but as will be discussed below, science has not provided sufficiently adequate answers in place of those once supplied by theology.

Using the question of legal authority as a case study, this chapter sketches the intellectual history of that concept in the West. "Legal authority" connotes the "'right to rule'; the exercise of which binds its subjects by imposing duties of obedience."[4] There is a standard, secular answer for legal authority today, but that answer does not adequately substitute for the earlier religious one. Several alternatives are being mooted in academic circles. In preference to those, the suggestion here is to turn to aesthetics. Aesthetics, the study of beauty, has become a major source for theology, providing a common approach for disparate religious orientations to common questions.[5] Aesthetics offers a similar promise for law in its need for alternatives to theological answers in the question of authority.

This discussion of law, theology, and aesthetics will use a method that reflects the interdisciplinary discussions between law and theology in CTI's Inquiry on Law and Religious Freedom. The aim is to forge a new path to resolving ancient issues that developed with the separation of two once closely related disciplines,

---

of Pennsylvania Press, 2015) and Winnifred Fallers Sullivan, *The Impossibility of Religious Freedom* (Princeton: Princeton University Press, 2005).

3. Within the Christian tradition, for example, Amish communities seek to organize all aspects of life according to their religious belief.

4. Samantha Besson, "The Authority of International Law—Lifting the Veil," *Sydney Law Review* 31 (2009): 343, 344, 345n2, citing Joseph Raz.

5. See, for example, Cyril O'Regan, "Theology, Art, and Beauty," in *The Many Faces of Beauty*, ed. V. Hösle (Notre Dame: University of Notre Dame Press, 2013), 445.

law and religion. In answering the question "Why should law have the power to command obedience of those subject to the law?" this essay will reflect on religious, aesthetic, and other answers, arguing for aesthetics as the approach that can bridge the long separation of law and religion in the West. Aesthetics is a compelling common source of insight to support the flourishing of humanity in community and in the natural world.

Authority, Theology, and Law

Currently, the most widely taught explanation of why law should be regarded as having authority is found in the Oxford legal philosopher H. L. A. Hart's classic 1961 book, *The Concept of Law*. Hart wrote that law depends on wide, voluntary acceptance as the reason that citizens can expect legal rules and principles to be obeyed. His explanation challenged the prevailing and still common view that law is the command of a sovereign backed by force.[6] Coercive enforcement or punishment is necessary for law, but must be the exception.[7] Acceptance is key. What Hart did not explain is how individuals and communities came to have this acceptance.

Some scholars find it sufficient to rely on intuition that law is good and should be accepted.[8] Intuition comes from somewhere, however. Standard histories of law in the West reveal the evolu-

6. H. L. A. Hart, *The Concept of Law* (Oxford: Oxford University Press, 1961).

7. Hart, *The Concept of Law*, 227.

8. See, for example, Tom Tyler, *Why People Obey the Law* (Princeton: Princeton University Press, 2006), 177–78: "Although people may decide to follow legal rules either from fear of punishment . . . or as a result of reasoning about the purpose of rules . . . most adults . . . have learned the value of following rules for their own sake. . . . This image differs strikingly from that of self-interest models which dominate current thinking in law, psychology, political science, sociology, and organizational theory." Social values continue to be shaped by religious and ethical commitments. See also Mark Greenberg, "The Moral Impact Theory of Law," *Yale Law Journal* 123 (2014): 1288.

tion of law and legal institutions from religious frameworks.[9] As late as the seventeenth century prominent legal scholars such as Hugo Grotius, a theologian and diplomat, said with confidence, "What God has shown to be his Will, that is law."[10] And if it is law, it must be obeyed. Yet, in an attempt to persuade Protestant and Catholic leaders to agree to the same version of international law, Grotius famously also wrote in the *Prolegomena to the Law of War and Peace* in 1625, "What we have been saying [about law] would have a degree of validity even if we should concede that which cannot be conceded without the utmost wickedness, that there is no God, or that the affairs of men are of no concern to him."[11] This formula developed over a long history. It was part of a movement to remove religion from politics and law in response to the "religio-political conflicts between Catholics and magisterial Protestants from the early sixteenth through the mid-seventeenth century":

> The solution eventually adopted in all modern, liberal Western states was to privatize religion and to distinguish it from public life, ideologically as well as institutionally, through politically protected rights to individual religious freedom. Not subjective faith but objective reason, in science and modern philosophy, could be the basis of public life. But modern states continued to rely on citizens' behaviors that depended on beliefs rooted in Christianity (such as individual rights) even as other cross-confessionally embraced behaviors (such as material acquisitiveness) were antithetical to its teachings.[12]

---

9. See, for example, Harold J. Berman, *Law and Revolution: The Formation of the Western Legal Tradition* (Cambridge, MA: Harvard University Press, 1983). Respecting international law, see Stephen Neff, *Justice Among Nations: A History of International Law* (Cambridge, MA: Harvard University Press, 2014), 5–136.

10. Hugo Grotius, *The Law of Prize*, chap. 2.

11. Grotius, *The Law of War and Peace*, Prolegomena, para. 11.

12. Gregory, *The Unintended Reformation*, 1.

For many decades, the European conception of law, exported through colonialism and other means throughout the world, continued to benefit from the centuries of association with divine authority. Law without God, however, slowly opened the door not only to secular law but also to law without authority above the sovereign. It was the sovereign that now had the right to make law drawing on his own internal resources, not the external divine or larger community. Each sovereign's interpretation of the law was as valid as another's. Emmerich de Vattel took from this understanding the conclusion that no state may sit in judgment of another.[13] Law came to be what the sovereign willed and not what was ordained by nature or the divine. Vattel helped pave the way for positivism to replace natural law. "Vattel's thinking was deeply embedded in the reasoning of the Enlightenment."[14] Law could be thought of separate from God. Individualism and sovereign absolutism were on the rise.[15] These developments, related to the rise of Protestantism, also fostered the scientific revolution and the premium placed on objective, material evidence.

Throughout the nineteenth century, European legal theorists attempted to demonstrate that law, including international law, was a branch of science, "legal science." Scholars sought to show that, as in other fields, "interrelated, fundamental and logically demonstrable principles of science" governed.[16] American law schools famously adopted "the case method" in the 1870s to educate lawyers in a way analogous to the education of scientists. Law students were—and still are—taught to look at the evidence in a judicial opinion to discover the rule, much as a botanist would study a plant to learn

13. Joachim von Elbe, "The Evolution of the Concept of the Just War in International Law," *American Journal of International Law* 33 (1939): 665, 682–83.

14. Philip Allott, *The Health of Nations* (Cambridge: Cambridge University Press, 2002), 56–62.

15. Mary Ellen O'Connell, *The Power and Purpose of International Law* (New York: Oxford University Press, 2008), 33–48.

16. Neil Duxbury, *Patterns of American Jurisprudence* (Oxford: Clarendon Press, 1995), 10.

the laws of nature. A great effort at classifying rules followed.[17] This arguably "objective" approach to law became known as formalism.[18] By the late nineteenth century, American legal realists challenged formalism for its artificiality. Law was not a science like botany. Indeed, proponents of legal realism such as Oliver Wendell Holmes viewed law as anything but science when he famously said that "law is what the courts say it is." Some in the legal realist movement, however, saw certain linkages between law and social science, especially economics. By the middle of the twentieth century, some looking beyond simpler notions of "legal science" began looking to economics. Law and economics and its variants, such as rational choice, public choice, and behavioral economics, is a widely held explanation for how law works, prominent in American law schools and increasingly beyond the United States. Other social sciences such as sociology, psychology, and anthropology became influential in law as well, but arguably not to the extent of economics.

In 2004, Stephen Smith examined the phenomenon of growing skepticism and uncertainty about the authority of law in the United States. He reviewed the various theories of authority from consent to public choice (law and economics) and concluded that none are adequate because none replaces the historic source of authority for law—God himself.[19] Smith reminds us that belief in law's authority is an inheritance from an age when legal scholars believed in God and in the ability to apply reason to understand what God ordained in the form of law. "Blackstone and Story were, after all, heirs of a worldview that assumed God was real—more real than anything else, in fact, or necessarily rather than contingently real—and had created the universe according to a providential plan. This view

17. C. C. Langdell, *A Selection of Cases on the Law of Contracts*, 2nd ed. (Boston: Little, Brown & Co., 1879), 1.

18. Jean d'Aspremont, *Formalism and the Sources of International Law: A Theory of the Ascertainment of Legal Rules* (Oxford: Oxford University Press, 2012).

19. Steven D. Smith, *Law's Quandary* (Cambridge, MA: Harvard University Press, 2004), 46–47.

had important implications for the nature of law."[20] Tradition can account to some extent for continuing belief in law. This inheritance has an existence of its own—our respect for law's authority today is a phenomenon in its own right.

Still, Smith may well have been right to sound the alarm about the declining respect for legal authority in a world no longer able to explain why law should be obeyed. Self-interest, the basis of economics-based theories of law compliance, does not explain cases of compliance in the absence of any benefit to self. The preferred explanation today, Hart's account of acceptance, both fails to acknowledge how acceptance evolved and, of greater concern, how acceptance remains robust. What happens should acceptance cease or habit change?

Theological Aesthetics and Law

Recently, theologians and philosophers concerned with the problem of law compliance and the authority of law have renewed the explanations from Christianity.[21] For many in the secular world of law, this direct approach is not persuasive. The interest in religion reveals an indirect approach, somewhere between wholly rejecting religion and wholly embracing it. The revival of aesthetics in the field of theology suggests the possibility of an aesthetic turn in law as well. The field of "theological aesthetics" "is concerned with questions about God and issues in theology in the light of and perceived through sense knowledge (sensation, feeling, imagina-

20. Smith, *Law's Quandary*; Gregory, *The Unintended Reformation*, 23.

21. For recent scholarly invocations of religion in interpreting contemporary legal theory, see Jeremy Waldron, "One Another's Equals: The Basis of Human Equality," Gifford Lectures 2014–2015, University of Edinburgh, http://www.gifford lectures.org/lectures/one-another's-equals-basis-human-equality (accessed November 8, 2016). See also Jean Porter, *Ministers of the Law: A Natural Law Theory of Legal Authority* (Grand Rapids: Eerdmans, 2010).

tion), through beauty, and the arts."[22] It is being embraced across the spectrum of Christian traditions and denominations. "This field of theology therefore is per se ecumenical." It can aid in the "search for Christian unity" as well as play a role "in fundamental theology in the more obvious area[s] of revelation and faith . . . dogmatics, scripture, church history, pastoral theology and ethics. Further, the dialogue between theology and the arts is 'ecumenical' in that it is an interdisciplinary endeavor."[23]

> Art, too, has an eschatological dimension since in art we can imagine and express the world as it could or should be. Indeed, one might claim that real art points us in the most diverse ways to a reality that could be and is not yet. . . .
>
> A world in need of redemption is a world in which the vision of God is not an optional extra. The vision of God constitutes the eschatological hope, the destination and goal of all followers of Christ and ultimately maybe of all human beings, as they are made in the image of God. The vision of God still attracts and awes people. Art, faith, theology, and doing the good, can provide paths to such glimpses of the transcendent.[24]

"Art points us in diverse ways to a reality that could be and is not yet," but can be pursued through art, religion, or law. Aesthetic theory teaches that these various paths can be combined or followed separately without conflict when all are paths to true beauty. The theologian Gordon Graham has written of the loss of faith and its effects on morality, saying that "without theological underpinnings morality is no more than convention and ethics just a kind of etiquette, [such that] one would expect the more heroic moral ideas to fall away and the role of positive law as a means of social regulation

22. Gesa Elsbeth Thiessen, *Theological Aesthetics: A Reader* (Grand Rapids: Eerdmans, 2004), 1.

23. Thiessen, *Theological Aesthetics*, 3–4.

24. Thiessen, *Theological Aesthetics*, 6.

to grow."[25] Law is often spoken of as a substitute for religion. Martti Koskenniemi has written: "Moral pathos and religion frequently fail as vocabularies of engagement, providers of 'empty signifiers' for expressing commitment and solidarity."[26] People look to such ideas as international law for a "vocabulary with a horizon of transcendence . . . a kind of secular faith."[27] Law can perhaps substitute for religion, religion for law, art for both, so long as the ultimate aim of each is the same.

Aesthetics and Legal Authority

It is possible to find common ground linking religion, law, and art in the support of harmonious life in community. All three approaches rely on proof that social life is a possible and attractive condition. This is where beauty is pivotal. Immanuel Kant wrote of the pleasure we experience when reflecting on what does not have utility. We experience pleasure in contemplating sunsets—actual or imagined—regardless of utility because of the beauty of the sunset. It is a very different experience than the pleasure of a fine wine or other luxuries. Iris Murdoch supplies an example of the power and reality of the human response to beauty.[28] She invites us to think of moments of self-concern, moments when we are focused on a perceived slight, a blow to our self-esteem. Then we look out the window and see an amazing bird, dancing along a tree branch. We experience pleasure triggered by a small example of beauty that does nothing practical for us. Such an experience of pleasure takes

25. Gordon Graham, *The Re-enchantment of the World* (Oxford: Oxford University Press, 2007), 44.

26. Martti Koskenniemi, "The Fate of Public International Law: Between Technique and Politics," *The Modern Law Review* 70 (January 2007): 1–30.

27. Koskenniemi, "The Fate of Public International Law," 30.

28. Iris Murdoch, *The Sovereignty of Good* (London: Routledge & Kegan Paul, 1970).

us out of ourselves—it is a disinterested pleasure, distinguishable from the pleasure of good food or a large house.

Hannah Arendt argues that Kant never wrote a theory or philosophy of politics or law.[29] Nevertheless, she finds in his *Critique of Judgment* evidence of at least the basis of a political theory. In my view that basis is also a basis for a theory of law. Arendt presented her case in a series of lectures at the New School for Social Research in 1970. Central to Arendt's understanding of Kant's political philosophy is what he says about beauty.[30] Kant suggested that a human being's happiness could not depend on experiencing pleasure alone. He thought the very ability to know pleasure depends on the contrast with displeasure. Arendt found in Kant "only one exception to this rule, and that is the pleasure we feel when confronted with beauty."[31] In perceiving true beauty, we experience a disinterested pleasure not dependent on any contrast. We perceive beauty and experience pleasure in the perception instinctually. "The fact that man is affected by the sheer beauty of nature proves that he is made for and fits into this world."[32] It creates the opposite sense to that of alienation from the world,[33] and is, therefore, a reason to be open to society.

Kant's real interest in beauty was even more directed to what it tells us about "disinterest" or interest in the other. Many beautiful things exist solely for their beauty and not because they have any usefulness for us. Thus, the pleasure is owing to the thing's mere existence and not for any gain. Arendt tells us that Kant wrote in a notebook, "the Beautiful teaches us to love without self-interest."[34] The beautiful and the disinterested pleasure experienced leads to a desire to communicate.[35] Communication in turn requires the abil-

29. Hannah Arendt, *Lectures on Kant's Political Philosophy*, ed. Ronald Beiner (Chicago: University of Chicago Press, 1992), 7–8.

30. Arendt, *Kant's Political Philosophy*, 30.

31. Arendt, *Kant's Political Philosophy*, 30.

32. Arendt, *Kant's Political Philosophy*, 30, quoting Kant.

33. Simon Swift, *Hannah Arendt* (London and New York: Routledge, 2009), 75.

34. Swift, *Hannah Arendt*, 73.

35. Swift, *Hannah Arendt*, 76.

ity to stand in the shoes of another, to have the enlarged mentality that reaches to a consideration of all humanity—the cosmopolitan perspective. Thus, in our experience of beauty we enjoy unselfish pleasure. The experience and the need to communicate about it lead us outside ourselves. And it is this thinking about being with others, "sociability," that is our "highest end."[36]

For Kant, the free play of imagination leads to a comprehension of what is beautiful. Beauty is different from what is simply agreeable and interesting in an object.[37] It is perceived as universal, not something unique to an individual's personal taste.[38] When we call something beautiful we think that everyone must recognize it as such, that everyone must agree with us. We desire consensus. Kant says that judging something to be beautiful "carries with it an aesthetic quality of universality."[39] As Terry Eagleton explains it, "we can experience our shared humanity with all the immediacy of our response to a fine painting or a magnificent symphony. Paradoxically, it is in the apparently most private, frail and intangible aspects of our lives that we blend most harmoniously with one another."[40]

Kant "lays out even more explicitly why it is that judgments about beauty tend simultaneously to exemplify and reinforce collective social judgments even when they do not overtly appear to do so."[41] This understanding of shared humanity and Arendt's extension to the wish for communication founds social life, and, therefore, political life. Social and political life being aspects of law,

---

36. Swift, *Hannah Arendt*, 76.

37. Immanuel Kant, *Critique of the Power of Judgment*, trans. Paul Guyer and Eric Matthews (Cambridge: Cambridge University Press, 1987), 97.

38. Kant, *Critique of Judgment*, 97: "With the beautiful it is entirely different. It would be ridiculous . . . if someone who prided himself on his taste thought to justify himself thus: 'This object . . . is beautiful for me.' For he must not call it beautiful if it please merely him."

39. Kant, *Critique of Judgment*, 101.

40. Swift, *Hannah Arendt*, 77, quoting Eagleton.

41. Mark Canuel, *Justice, Dissent, and the Sublime* (Baltimore: Johns Hopkins University Press, 2012), 30.

Arendt's insight can be extended to the reason for law. Law supports social peace, harmony, and order. Arendt quotes Kant but uses as many of her own words: "[I]f everyone expects and requires from everyone else this reference to general communication [of pleasure, of disinterested delight, then we have reached a point where it is as if there existed] an original compact, dictated by mankind itself."[42]

Mark Canuel finds Arendt's argument really her own and not Kant's. "The idea of the aesthetic as a political means of joining individuals through a *sensus communis* becomes crucial in Hannah Arendt's interpretation of Kant's aesthetics and its implication for his politics. Arendt quite clearly anticipates the work of Guyer and Connolly in viewing the aesthetic as a 'common sense' producing a 'standard of communicability.'"[43] He believes that Arendt is closer to Schiller than to Kant, given Kant's preference for the political aesthetic of the sublime versus the beautiful. Canuel argues that Kant found in the sublime the motivation to dissent and contestation, which he believes is necessary to achieve justice. For Kant, according to Canuel, "Justice as equal treatment before the law requires the engagement and testing of contrary standpoints, demands, and needs."[44] Other followers of Kant, such as John Rawls, also stress the centrality of justice and the role of contested politics to achieve it. That is not Arendt's understanding, however. Canuel finds her far closer to Schiller than Kant in emphasizing beauty as the foundational concept of social life, not the sublime.

Beauty suggests harmony, communication, and understanding of the common sense of the world. Canuel is right that beauty does not celebrate contestation but rather resolution. In this, beauty supports law as the alternative to brute force or unregulated violence to resolve disputes. Contestation that is resolved by violence is the antithesis of social life, certainly social life based on the need to communicate. Nonviolent, peaceful resolution of disputes through

42. Swift, *Hannah Arendt*, 74.
43. Canuel, *Justice, Dissent, and the Sublime*, 52n32.
44. Canuel, *Justice, Dissent, and the Sublime*, 52n42.

law fosters Augustine's "tranquility in order."[45] As will be discussed in the next section, the very rules that foster peace and suppress violence reflect the equality, fairness, and justice that form the heart of the law as validated through the insights of aesthetics.

The insight about beauty indicates a yet more important empirical fact. Beyond the need to communicate to truly experience the pleasure of beauty, the experience is common to people. All human beings experience this pleasure, which has no apparent purpose. The blind experience beauty through music or imagination. It is a pure aspect of our common humanity, which supplies a far more tangible basis for empathy, for seeing the other as ourselves, than that supplied by the concept of human dignity, the existence of a soul, or the fact of common needs. The pleasure in experiencing beauty is a universal, harmonious, and noncompetitive aspect of humanity.

Founding social life on Hume's pleasure principle is far more challenging than Kant's, given the zero-sum nature of the commodities that supply self-interested pleasure. People compete for wealth and what it provides. Common needs, which so often form the content of theories of the common good, require sacrifice to fulfill. People need food, water, accommodation, even love and play. We certainly see commonality in these needs that can lead to empathy, but we also see at the same time that the acquisition of these things for me means less for you. Even love, which is associated with altruism, is deficient for Murdoch in that "human love is normally too profoundly possessive and also too 'mechanical' to be a place of vision."[46]

The great economic and social theories have tried to overcome the essential competitive aspect of human need. Communism and Christianity teach from each according to his or her ability, to each

45. Quincy Wright uses this expression in explaining the purpose of law. "It is the function of law to produce this condition." See Quincy Wright, *A Study of War* (Chicago: University of Chicago Press, 1964), 173–74.
46. Murdoch, *Sovereignty of Good*, 84.

according to his or her need. Capitalism teaches to each according to ability and more will be created for all. The emphasis on ability in all of these creeds is a focus on a human characteristic that is distributed differently to different people, inspiring hierarchy and competition. In contrast, people can have the common experience of pleasure in a rose in first bloom, a sunset, or a Da Vinci portrait. In Hume's theory a person theoretically needs no social life. Kant and Arendt see in the perception of beauty the truth of social life as integral to human existence. Why else have the experience of beauty?

We have largely lost this vocabulary and understanding from our political and jurisprudential thought. The question is whether it can be recovered. By this point in the argument, some might wonder whether there really is a common experience of beauty ("beauty is in the eye of the beholder"). Others might question whether the common experience of beauty can do much for law. It is true that *taste* differs among people. Someone credited with "good taste" often has a combination of talent and training and may have a more profound experience of beauty. The intensity of the experience of beauty differs. That fact does not, however, diminish the common ability of all people to experience some level of disinterested pleasure in beauty. Aesthetic pleasure is an extraordinary thing to have in common, and for those still skeptical, there is a wealth of scientific evidence to support what Plato, Aristotle, and Thomas Aquinas concluded without brain scans or surveys.

David Novak, in a chapter on Jewish natural law, writes, "Th[e] active discovery of authentic human nature and its requirements comes when practical or moral reason is properly exercised. It is not discovered by contemplation of the beauty of the external world."[47] The observation reveals a misunderstanding of what the philosophers tell us may be gained by contemplation of beauty. Contempla-

47. Anver Emon et al., *Natural Law: A Jewish, Christian, and Muslim Trialogue* (Oxford: Oxford University Press, 2014), 8.

tion of beauty reveals a common fact of human experience, which is an experience of disinterested pleasure. This is not a revelation about human nature as much as a revelation of a human capacity, an intuition or reaction of the senses.

We find in Murdoch an example of Novak's point. She applies practical and moral reason to conclude something about human nature: It is naturally selfish.[48] She then builds moral philosophy around antidotes for selfishness. "Following a hint in Plato (Phaedrus 250) I shall start by speaking of what is perhaps the most obvious thing in our surroundings which is an occasion for 'unselfing', and that is what is popularly called beauty."[49] "Plato pointed out, beauty is the only spiritual thing which we love by instinct."[50] Murdoch offers a gloss on Kant's experience of disinterested pleasure in contemplation of the beautiful. She accepts that this experience may be produced through contemplation of good art. The surer object for the experience of unselfish pleasure, however, is nature. "[W]e take a self-forgetful pleasure in the sheer alien pointless independent existence of animals, birds, stones and trees. 'Not how the world is, but that it is is the mystical.'"[51]

The good life is the unselfish life. This becomes known through the unselfish pleasure experienced in the contemplation of beauty, especially in nature. "The self, the place where we live, is a place of illusion. Goodness is connected with the attempt to see the unself, to see and to respond to the real world in the light of a virtuous consciousness."[52]

Elaine Scarry provides insights that further develop the propositions about politics offered by Arendt. Scarry's insights are particularly helpful in extending Arendt's understanding beyond politics to law. Scarry, drawing on Plato, Dante, Simone Weil, Murdoch,

---

48. Murdoch, *Sovereignty of Good*, 78.
49. Murdoch, *Sovereignty of Good*, 84.
50. Murdoch, *Sovereignty of Good*, 84
51. Murdoch, *Sovereignty of Good*, 85.
52. Murdoch, *Sovereignty of Good*, 93.

and others, sees the perception of beauty drawing us from the contemplation of a particular beautiful thing to the general, the universal. Care for one thing of beauty leads to care and concern for the world.[53]

Relevant to the question of the ground for the authority of law, Scarry informs us of the linguistic, historic, and conceptual links between beauty and justice. "Beauty" and "fairness" were once used interchangeably. As Aristotle taught, fairness is the equal application of the law, which is a definition of justice. For Augustine, "equality is the morally highest and best feature of the world."[54] Equality, proportion, symmetry are at the heart of beauty. Or in the thinking of Thomas Aquinas, beauty has the characteristics of clarity, integrity, and proportion. Beauty in its proportion and symmetry exerts "pressure" toward ethical equality.[55] Beauty in its proportion persuades us instinctually of the rightness of fair law. Achieving justice through law that treats people equally is valued. We accept the value of treating people equally in the law, an acceptance supported by our instinctual interest in the other. Being drawn outside ourselves to the world by its beauty supports our interest and empathy.

Scarry cites Weil and Murdoch for the "radical decentering we undergo in the presence of the beautiful." The attention focused on one's self is released, freeing one to turn one's focus toward others.[56] Beauty does more than alter our perspective. According to Scarry, it inspires action, including action toward justice, which is, again, toward equality of treatment.[57] Scarry rightly sees "that beauty's emphasis on symmetry, communicability, and shared emotion provides a model for ideal social relations, relations described in terms

53. Elaine Scarry, *On Beauty and Being Just* (Princeton: Princeton University Press, 1999), 82.
54. Scarry, *Beauty and Being Just*, 98.
55. Scarry, *Beauty and Being Just*, 109.
56. Scarry, *Beauty and Being Just*, 113.
57. Scarry, *Beauty and Being Just*, 115.

of justice or mutuality."[58] Justice or mutuality requires a sense of commonality and harmony among beings.

The inspiration needed to bring just arrangements into being can be found according to Philip Allott through contemplation of the ideal, also referred to as "excellence" or "the beautiful." As he explains, "[T]he mind contains a particular kind of idea—the ideal—a powerful form of mental energy that leads us to make a *better* reality caused by the magnetic attraction of ideas such as justice, the good, the true, the beautiful, the ideal."[59]

Aesthetics as a foundation of legal authority is offered here as a new concept to found contemporary international law. The relationship of beauty to political and legal theory is understandable to the extent that moral and legal structures have an aesthetic component. In addition, however, beauty and theories about beauty fire the imagination, "which communicates the 'vision' of the theorist."[60] Canuel, however, argues that the vision created by the beautiful lacks the "sense of disagreement" essential to a theory of "political justice."[61]

Canuel rejects the logic of beauty with its support for association and justice as recognition, beauty's defense "in the name of justice, equality or mutuality."[62] His position seems right that the sublime encourages disagreement, individual desire, and emphasis on particularity as opposed to commonality. Canuel assumes that a healthy appreciation of the beautiful already exists in the form of shared frameworks to contain and cabin the disagreement

58. Canuel, *Justice, Dissent, and the Sublime*, 5.

59. Philip Allott, "The Idealist's Dilemma." Remarks presented at the International Law Association (British Branch) Spring Conference, King's College, Inner Temple, London, May 23–24, 2014.

60. Canuel, *Justice, Dissent, and the Sublime*, 7.

61. Canuel, *Justice, Dissent, and the Sublime*, 7. He wants to associate with John Rawls's theory of justice, which is based on impartiality. To do so, Canuel finds in Rawls allowances for the partiality supported by the sublime.

62. Canuel, *Justice, Dissent, and the Sublime*, 39.

and conflict he seeks.[63] He critiques beauty theory as too dominant—calling for too much harmony and passivity. This hardly
seems to be a problem in law, where the field seems to have jumped
over beauty and alighted on acceptance of contestation as a virtue.
Along these lines, Canuel advocates drawing on the aesthetic of
the sublime.

The suppression of beauty theory from legal theory is related
to Protestant individualism, iconoclasm, and the move to Enlightenment positivism seeking to substitute science for religion to
explain legal authority. By the time Grotius wrote about international law in a way that separated law and religion, Protestant
theologians had already dismissed the emphasis on beauty in art
and nature as a path to God. Costas Douzinas reminds us that
the connection between beauty and law was once well known and
continues to be represented in the attractive, blindfolded statues
of justice, holding a sword in one hand and balance in the other.
He points to "the inner relationship between the beautiful and
the good," noting that, "the link between law, order, and harmony,
or between justice and beauty forms a consistent theme in the
writings of the humanist lawyers both in England and continental
Europe."[64] The Reformation and Protestant iconoclasm took a toll
on thinking about beauty at the heart of law. The Protestant focus

---

63. His focus seems to be within the state, especially the United States, and
the state of the American university. His observations have resonance as he points
to the corporatization of US universities, seen "in the academy's shift from an emphasis on public criticism to 'industrial management,' from independent inquiry
to partnerships between 'research institutions and the business community.'" See
Canuel, *Justice, Dissent, and the Sublime*, 34, citing Masao Miyoshi, "Globalization,
Culture, and the University," in *The Cultures of Globalization*, ed. Frederic Jameson
and Masao Miyoshi (Durham, NC: Duke University Press, 1998), 264. It seems
right to warn as he does of the influence of beauty on engendering passivity. Still,
he fails to connect the rise of corporate power in the interest of the few as the clear
triumph of the sublime's power aesthetic stripped of beauty's concern for equality
and community.

64. Costas Douzinas and Lynda Nead, eds., *Law and the Image: The Authority
of Art and the Aesthetics of Law* (Chicago: University of Chicago Press, 1999), 53.

moves to text and music and away from the visual and performative. Kant considered the Old Testament condemnation of "graven images" as "sublime."[65]

Kierkegaard provides a serious argument for moving aesthetics outside of the church to a narrower focus on art, a move supported by Nietzsche who sees the arts as a substitute for God.[66] Nietzsche argues that through the arts one can have a spiritual experience without religion. Far from foreclosing all religious belief, this sort of thinking provides respectability to a certain kind of religiosity, even among highly educated Europeans. Religious belief results in spiritual experience, experience that inspires the greatest work of visual, literary, and performative art. Theologians eventually return to aesthetics (famously with Hans Urs von Balthasar) because the link between beauty and spirituality was never lost.[67]

The theologian Bruno Forte explains that the fear of the beautiful in our times coincides with the certainty of death. Beauty has clarity, integrity, and proportion. The favorite example of beauty, the rose in new bloom, indicates all three. All three will soon be lost—the rose's color will fade; brown spots will appear; the petals will curl and drop off, leaving a lopsided memory of what was. The rose will die. The beauty of the new rose imparts disinterested pleasure but also the reality of death. "Here we can grasp why beauty unsettles us in a way we often seek to avoid: we flee from beauty as we flee from the thought of death. And this is indeed not only the experience of individuals, but also of humankind and of whole epochs."[68] A return to beauty is to return to reality and its possibility of transcendence—the true escape from death.

65. Canuel, *Justice, Dissent, and the Sublime*, 47.

66. Graham, *The Re-enchantment of the World*.

67. Thiessen, *Theological Aesthetics*, 1.

68. Bruno Forte, *The Portal of Beauty: Towards a Theology of Aesthetics* (Grand Rapids: Eerdmans, 2008), 114–15.

Conclusion

The aesthetic theory of beauty reveals a way to think about legal authority without directly invoking the commands of the divine to obey law. Beauty takes us out of ourselves and gives us a reason to accept law for the good of others, not just ourselves. This is a reason beyond narrow self-interest, which is where we are left in relying on economic theories of law alone. If law is to succeed in its most important task of controlling violence, it needs the answers aesthetic theory provides as to why obey law.

Legal scholars can follow the lead of other disciplines in finding answers in the aesthetic theory of the beautiful. The return to aesthetics in Western thought is renewing theology, philosophy, and the sciences. It can do the same for law.

A Collaborative Manner of Theological Reflection

DOUGLAS F. OTTATI

I did not participate in the Center of Theological Inquiry project between 2012 and 2015 but was later invited to listen in and reflect on conversations among those who did. I did so with a specific question in mind: Was the three-year Inquiry project representative of an identifiable manner of theological reflection? I concluded that it was, and my aim here is to describe the sort of theology the Inquiry project represented and distinguish it from some prominent contemporary alternatives.

There were reasons to think the project as a whole might not be sufficiently coherent to represent an identifiable mode of theologizing. Participants represented different disciplines and fields—everything from evolutionary biology, neuroscience, anthropology, and the history of law to theology. Their own scholarly projects were also quite diverse. One was developing new neuroscientific models of the role of affect, emotions, or feelings in moral behavior. Another worked to reconstruct a Christian realist perspective in theological ethics. A third investigated cognitive underpinnings of religious conversion, with particular attention to the apostle Paul. Yet another investigated competing conceptions of the right to religious freedom in different societies and raised questions about its neutrality and secularity. Moreover, the theologians who partici- pated in the seminars represented a variety of Christian traditions, including Roman Catholic, Reformed, and Methodist.

A Collaborative Sensibility

Even so, much was shared between participants. Whether they were discussing evolution and human nature, religion and psychology, or law and religious freedom, what brought the participants together was a program of multidisciplinary research. In each Inquiry, people trained in different disciplines and fields met to discuss a common topic with the aim of enriching and advancing their own under- standing as anthropologists, psychologists, neuroscientists, histori- ans, physicists, cosmologists, biologists, legal experts, theologians, and just plain people. They were sometimes led to reconsider and revise their own reflections as well as their approaches to their own disciplines. Occasionally, they concluded that their own discipline it- self needed not only supplementing but also revising in conjunction with the contributions of those operating with other frameworks. As one participant put it, "When you try to understand how another discipline or field approaches a subject, you see your own discipline anew." Thus, in each Inquiry, the participants shared a common in- terest in the topic under discussion. They also shared a rough and ready conviction that, though they operated with different meth- odologies and vocabularies, their conversations might be mutually enriching and might even converge on an understanding of the topic richer and more nuanced than they had thought possible.

The willingness to believe it may be fruitful to engage in con- versations about relatively common topics with people who employ different disciplinary frameworks is what I shall call *a collaborative sensibility*. Not unique to programs at CTI, it is becoming increas- ingly common in our current intellectual milieu.

Recall the introductory essay's suggestion that with the rise of modern disciplines a new kind of inquiry took hold. Unlike the great medieval and Reformation theological systems, it did not aim at a comprehensive vision of reality but focused instead on specific kinds of information. By means of rigorous methods of investigation and analysis, the information was organized into discrete bodies of evidence. The evidence, in turn, supported theories, and both the evidence and the theories could be tested by anyone with the same specialized competence.

The disciplines set limits on what could be known, and large parts of what earlier philosophy and theology claimed to explore, e.g. metaphysics, were to be dismissed as incomprehensible. In return the disciplines promised a new universality and certainty—anyone anywhere who underwent appropriate specialized training could test their evidence and conclusions. They also promised a heightened, almost industrial productivity, as knowledge became the collective work of a multitude of organized investigators. The benefits, from physics and chemistry to biology, psychology, the social sciences, and even the humanities, were tremendous. Nevertheless, in recent decades, many have come to appreciate important limits to disciplinary thinking, and as a result research centers, universities, and colleges increasingly have brought together specialized researchers to reflect about common problems, topics, and ideas.

The new mood may have been felt first at think tanks and ethics centers that brought together information and ideas from different quarters in order to probe difficult questions of morality and policy in medicine, urban planning, population growth, and so on. But for some years now it has also made itself felt in college and university curricula. Thus, one notes the proliferation of interdisciplinary and also "transdisciplinary" courses, departments, and majors. At Davidson College, for example, there is a Center for Interdisciplinary Studies, through which students may propose majors that draw on more than one academic department. There are interdisciplinary minors, such as East Asian Studies, and there are also multidisciplinary departments, such as Africana Studies and Environmental Studies—the latter of which draws on professors of economics, English, anthropology, biology, chemistry, religion, and political science.[1] Consider, too, the comparatively new field of astrobiology, which addresses basic questions about life on Earth as well as habitable environments and the possibilities for microbial and others forms of life elsewhere in the universe. NASA describes it as drawing on broadly "interdisciplinary research in molecular biology, ecology, planetary science, astronomy, information science, space exploration technologies, and related disciplines."[2]

The collaborative sensibility exhibited by the CTI seminars reflects a newer interdisciplinary and multidisciplinary intellectual circumstance following upon an era of highly differentiated, sometimes also insular methods and disciplinary self-understandings. CTI clearly is also not the only place where Christian theologians enter into conversations with representatives of other, nontheological disciplines and fields.[3] But because the Inquiries at CTI are places where Christian theologians enter into sustained interdisciplinary conversations, they raise the question of what the new collaborative sensibility may mean for Christian theology.

1. In addition, the Graduate School of the University of North Carolina at Chapel Hill maintains "transdisciplinary programs" that offer dual degrees in different disciplines, joint degrees from two or more different UNC institutions, and single degrees for courses in multiple disciplines.

2. David J. Des Marias, Joseph A. Nuth III, et al., "The NASA Astrobiology Roadmap," *Astrobiology* 8, no. 4 (2008): 715.

3. For example, there is also the Center for Theology and Natural Sciences affiliated with the Graduate Theological Union in Berkeley, CA, and its journal *Theology and Science*, as well as the Research Center for International and Interdisciplinary Theology at Heidelberg University.

Christian Theology

Today's interdisciplinary and multidisciplinary intellectual circumstances present Christian theologians with opportunities for a more collaborative manner of envisioning God, the world, and ourselves. To understand how this is so, however, we need to say something about what Christian theology is and does.

At the outset, for example, it should be said there are important respects in which Christian theology is *not* a discipline or field of inquiry like many other modern disciplines and fields, such as sociology, law, or environmental studies. One reason this is so is that the reflective activity called Christian theology inquires about a rather peculiar object, i.e., God and other things in relation to God. Peculiarity is signaled by the fact that the divine is not an object alongside of other objects and is not known as other objects are.[4] We cannot point to God as we might a tree or a bumblebee. We cannot weigh and measure God as we might weigh and measure a Toyota sedan. So, if you see the following sequence on your spiritual SATs—Africa, rock, frog, Pentagon, God, stock exchange, galaxy—the one that, in many respects, does not belong is God.

Moreover, the general claim is that the deity, who remains beyond all things, is experienced and known in and through our encounters with the world of objects and events. Thus, we encounter divine wisdom in our interactions with the created world, but the creation is not God. The Israelites encounter God in and through their escape from Egypt, their wanderings in the wilderness, and their constitution as a nation. But their escape is not God; neither are their wanderings or their formation as a nation.

Peculiarity is signaled, too, by the claim that God is Creator of all. This means that, as it investigates this object, Christian theology is driven to reflect on *all* things in relation to God. It therefore

---

4. James M. Gustafson, *Ethics from a Theocentric Perspective* (Chicago: University of Chicago Press, 1981), vol. 1.

maintains a capacious or panoramic intent at odds with the earlier specialized and discrete pictures of what a modern discipline should be. Indeed, a collaborative impulse seems built in to the basic terms of the theological enterprise and its drive to interpret objects, situations, and realities that may also be interpreted in nontheological terms. Thomas Aquinas says that theology or holy teaching (*sacra doctrina*) expresses judgments about God and creatures in relation to God.[5] H. Richard Niebuhr's radical monotheism situates humanity in the midst of the community of all being with God at its head, and James M. Gustafson regards theology as an attempt to understand all things in their appropriate relations with God.[6]

We might say that a statement, set of statements, or discourse is theological if it has to do with God and with other things in relation to God. Relatedness to God is what unifies theological reflections somewhat like relatedness to society, social structures, and practices is what unifies sociology. But God remains peculiar, and there is nothing that is not related to God in some way.

Theology, Church, and Interpreting the World

Now for a second (and related) point—as they reflect on God and other things in relation to God, Christian theologians are representatives of the church. They are, as John Calvin put it, teachers in the church, or as we might say, they are furthering an inquiry that is supported by the church.[7] One thing this means is that Christian theologians make use of and are guided by insights furnished

5. Thomas Aquinas, *Summa theologiae* I, 1, 7.

6. H. Richard Niebuhr, *Radical Monotheism and Western Culture with Supplementary Essays* (Louisville: Westminster John Knox, 1993), 31–37, 86–89; James M. Gustafson, "Say Something Theological!" (The Nora and Edward Ryerson Lecture at the University of Chicago, April 25, 1981).

7. John Calvin, *Institutes of the Christian Religion*, trans. Ford Lewis Battles (Louisville: Westminster John Knox, 1960), 4.1.5 (pp. 1016–20).

by the historic tradition of a particular religious community. They reflect on human beings and all other things in relation to the God disclosed in Jesus Christ as testified to in the Bible, and they are in conversation with the reflections of others who have done this at other times and places (the theological tradition). The appeals to God in Christ and to the theological heritages of Christian communities signal the irreducibly historical and particular dimensions of Christian theological inquiry. Christian theologians reflect on all things in relation to God, but the God in relation to whom they interpret all things is the Creator-Redeemer apprehended in the particular story of Israel and Jesus Christ.

The particular religious community called church carries out the reflective activity called Christian theology as it pursues its practical interest in forming people so that they may respond faithfully to God in the midst of their interactions with objects and others. That is, the church has a pastoral interest in helping people interact with families, possessions, governments, forests, animals, and more in a manner that is influenced and informed by devotion to God. This is where theology comes in. The church tries to build people up in a faithful way of living, and Christian theology presents a vision of God and world, or of the context for meaningful human life, that accompanies and informs this way of living. It articulates a practical wisdom and worldview that informs Christian practice and devotion.

A primary purpose of the church, then, is to deepen, promote, and extend a certain pattern of sensibility and devotion, or a piety, and thus build up the people of God in a life of faithfulness. It does this by means of a variety of practices, from worship and preaching to instruction, fellowship, care, and mission. But the critical point for our purposes is that the enterprise of pastoral formation, or of building up people in a piety and faithful way of living, also requires reflective activity. This is so because, generally speaking, the way we envision and interpret an object, situation, or reality influences our disposition toward it and our responses to it.

For example, those who pictured the Soviet Union as an evil empire were disposed to dislike, fear, and oppose its communist regime. Those who envision the current global circumstance with the aid of the image of a clash of civilizations may be disposed to dislike, fear, and oppose particular cultures and religious traditions. Christian theology helps to shape and express our sensibilities and attitudes toward objects and others by encouraging us to envision them with the aid of the symbolic idea of God in Christ. By envisioning objects and others in this manner, it helps to train people in a piety or fundamental disposition toward God and other things in relation to God.

Consider the Earth. We live on it and appreciate it. Sometimes, we fear its forces, and its beauty and sublimity may inspire awe. We also alter the Earth and often despoil it. A Christian theological vision will portray the Earth as God's good creation. This means, among other things, that the Earth, good in its several parts, is very good as an ensemble or as an interrelated whole.[8] Theologically speaking, the Earth is a gift, a divine donation, yet it is not simply ours to do with as we please. Why? Because the Earth remains the Lord's. Its ensemble has a kind of integrity, and it constitutes a sustaining habitat on which both we and other creatures depend. It is a world in which we are graced to participate by deploying our distinctive created capacities for appreciation and intervention, and for which we therefore have distinctive responsibilities as stewards.

By introducing images such as "God's creation" and "gift of God," Christian theology pictures the world and ourselves in relation to God. It introduces the distinctive relationship between ourselves, the Earth, and God that emerges in the Bible and Christian tradition. Remember that in many legal contexts, if I give you something, then it really is yours to do with as you please. By contrast, the image of the world as a "gift of God" makes us stewards accountable

8. Augustine, *The Confessions*, trans. Maria Boulding, OSB, vol. I/1 of *The Works of Saint Augustine: A Translation for the 21st Century*, ed. John E. Rotelle (Hyde Park, NY: New City Press, 1997), 373–76.

to the giver. This picture, in turn, evokes certain emotions, e.g., thankfulness and gratitude, and it informs our attempts to interact with the Earth in a manner that is also faithfully responsive to God.

What Collaboration Entails

Christian theology, then, may be described as a practical wisdom that articulates a vision of God, the world, and ourselves in the service of a particular piety, settled disposition, and way of living. As such, it construes God in relation to the many objects and others with which we interact. It develops a worldview, a vision of God and world or of the total context for meaningful human life in the service of Christian faithfulness, and so has a kind of panoramic or comprehensive interest that discrete modern disciplines often do not.

Indeed, there is a history of theological reasoning and inquiry about the varied objects, situations, and realities Christians encounter that tries to equip them to lead lives of faithfulness in their own places and times. This is one way to understand Augustine's magnificent and rambling *City of God*; it tries to equip Christians and their communities to lead faithful lives in face of the fall of Rome. In any case, the inquiry called Christian theology aims to develop a practical wisdom, and it assumes that, in order to be practically wise, one should be broadly informed about God and other things in relation to God.

What, then, does it mean for Christian theologians to adopt a collaborative sensibility something like the one required for contemporary multidisciplinary inquiries and conversations? Basically, it means being open and responsive to conversations with other, nontheological disciplines and fields in the conviction that these conversations may help to clarify, develop, revise, and improve one's theological reflections. For example, to return to the previous illustration, it means asking how the astrophysicist's finding that Earth is one planet among millions in a galaxy among millions of galaxies impacts a Christian theological portrait of God's good creation. Again, what does it mean for theological estimates of the human creature when biologists and primatologists point out that humans are, in many respects, much like other animals, and that some of our prized social and moral sensibilities may have homologues in other primates?[9] Or, again, what may it mean for Christian ethics when some philosophers argue that human agency operates at the intersection of mundane desires and the directives of moral law? Can conversations about matters such as these help theologians to engage certain features of their biblical and theological traditions that were largely neglected or even suppressed during the period of modern industrialism? Might they also help theologians to construct revised, enriched, and perhaps also truer visions of God's creation and our place in it than we sometimes find in the church's theological traditions?

This is where the intellectual virtues of humility and hope become especially relevant. Humility entails a sense for the incompleteness not only of one's own reflections but also (potentially) of one's own discipline or field. The theologian who enters into collaborative discussions will need to admit that her or his Christian theological framework does not have an unchallenged access to a comprehensive "theory of everything" that displaces all other approaches and interpretative vocabularies. It too is incomplete and subject to malformations; otherwise, there is no genuine motive for multidisciplinary discussions and comparative inquiries.

For Christian theologians, the measure of humility needed to support a felt sense of incompleteness will be associated with a strong sense for the transcendence, mystery, and incomprehensibility of the only and sovereign God who creates and redeems. Thus, to some extent and degree, God and world (or the whole of reality)

---

9. Frans de Waal et al., *Primates and Philosophers: How Morality Evolved*, ed. Stephen Macedo and Josiah Ober (Princeton: Princeton University Press, 2006), 161–81.

must always remain mysterious. This feature of what is sometimes called negative theology correlates with the conviction that our experience and knowledge are limited, partial, and subject to revision and correction. Finite humans never achieve an absolute perspective on life, history, faith, or reality. Indeed, resident in the sense of incompleteness and fallibility is an appreciation not only for our finitude but also our sin. Limited persons and communities (ourselves most certainly among them) are prone to place themselves at the center of things. As a result, human knowledge and faith are mired in a chronic pretension to be more than they are—though finite and limited by particular perspectives at particular places and times, they often pretend to be ultimate and final.[10] Thus, it very well may be that inter- and multidisciplinary conversations contribute an important check on the hubris of religious communities and theologians.

Humility, as the introductory essay to this volume also makes plain, will be paired with the intellectual virtue of hope, an anticipation that interdisciplinary discussion may enhance our knowledge and understanding. Indeed, for Christian theologians, hope is positively linked with humility. For, theologically speaking, if it is true that our limited and partial perspectives always fall short of finality and complete comprehension, it is nevertheless also true that, by the grace of God, the world as creation is not simply chaotic, but an ordered and sustaining environment that humans can probe and know. By grace as well, the God who creates also admonishes, corrects, redeems, and renews even the inquiries and visions of pretentious and misguided humans. This is why, in a Christian frame of reference, there is always reason to hope that human knowledge and understanding may make significant advances.

Even so, in the light of what we said earlier about Christian theology and the particular community called church, its scriptures

10. Reinhold Niebuhr, *The Nature and Destiny of Man* (New York: Scribner's, 1941), 1:217.

and traditions, we need to make a further point. Wherever Christian theologians take up a collaborative sensibility, they also experience *tension* between being open and hopeful about genuine change and revision, on the one hand, and preserving the particular integrity of Christian believing and theology, on the other. Collaborative theologians walk a fine line. They try to adopt a "being-open-without-losing-one's-sense-for-the-integrity-of-the-theological-enterprise" position as well as a "being-concerned-for-the-particularity-and-depth-of-Christian-theology-without-becoming-overly-dogmatic" position. They are against merely setting Christian theology and other disciplines in parallel so that they neither intersect nor challenge one another. They are interested in terms such as "transdisciplinarity," which point to important respects in which one's own interpretative or disciplinary framework may be altered, revised, or transformed in conversations with representatives of other frameworks. But they also worry about too ready and too easy syntheses of Christian theology with the current findings and theories of other disciplines.

It is true, of course, that one may mitigate the risk that things will go wrong by submitting one's work for review in both church and society, but the risk cannot be eliminated. Hierarchical church authorities, put in place partly to ensure the particular integrity of Christian believing, sometimes demand that theological reflection be insulated from serious challenges. Likewise, impulses simply to accommodate Christian theology to contemporary theories and ideas run especially strong in some secularly minded colleges and universities. The risk that the balance may fail must be recognized as a feature of collaborative theologizing on the boundary between Christian theology and other disciplines, between the church's historically specific insight and the world's knowledge.[11] In the end,

---

11. Paul Tillich wrote that "the concept of the boundary might be the fitting symbol for the whole" of his "personal and intellectual development," and that "the boundary is the best place for acquiring knowledge." *On the Boundary: An Autobiographical Sketch* (New York: Charles Scribner's Sons, 1966), 13.

there is no substitute for the theologian's venture of genuine engagement and disciplined judgment.

A Particular Pattern of Christian Convictions

A collaborative manner of theologizing is responsive to the contemporary multidisciplinary intellectual climate; one may even argue that it is partly a way for theology to catch up with intellectual life in contemporary colleges and universities. But as I intimated earlier, it has also made its presence felt in the history of theological reflection. More specifically, a collaborative manner of theologizing also has roots in a specific pattern of Christian convictions that comes to expression in important representatives of Roman Catholic, Anglican, Lutheran, Reformed, and Methodist Christian subtraditions. The pattern sets out basic terms for a Christian wisdom or worldview, and is analogous to a disciplinary framework of interpretation. With variations, it comes to expression in Augustine, Thomas Aquinas, Martin Luther, John Calvin, John Wesley, F. D. Maurice, and others.

The key conviction is that in Christ, God is Creator and Redeemer. John 1, which says all things came into being through the Word of God that has now redemptively become flesh, is among the scripture passages often cited in support. So is Colossians 1, which claims that God reconciles to Godself all things (*ta panta*) by means of the Lord Jesus Christ through and for whom all things have been created. Paul's statement in 2 Corinthians 5 furnishes something of a summary. God was in Christ reconciling the world to Godself; "in Christ, there is a new creation . . . see, everything has become new."

This, of course, does not mean that all mystery is dispelled. First Timothy 6:16 says that God dwells in unapproachable light, and many classical theologians, including Thomas Aquinas and the Protestant writers of the Scots Confession of 1560 and the Westminster Confession of Faith (1647), testify that the deity remains incomprehensible.[12] Nevertheless, there is genuine content to the apprehension of God in Christ. If God is Creator and Redeemer, then the world and all that is in it belongs to the God who creates and redeems. The creation is God's good gift, an ordered and sustaining environment that God chooses to renew and save.

Additional convictions are situated and understood within this frame of reference. For example, the reconciliation and redemption of all things indicates a need for grace and renewal, and thus the presence of a skewing corruption. Augustine therefore emphasizes a second feature of this particular pattern of Christian conviction when he insists that the whole person (heart, mind, and will) is corrupted and that all persons and institutions, including the church, suffer from sin's misdirection.[13] But since, for Augustine, God's creating and redeeming activity takes priority, humans and the world are misdirected or corrupted *goods* rather than simply evil or entirely opposed to God. Indeed, as Maurice understood it, they are on their way toward redemption because the fullness of God in Christ forms the basis for Christ's universal kingship and the redeeming adoption of all into fellowship with God.[14] In Christ, "all things were created to live with God and each other" in a reconciled community.[15]

---

12. Aquinas, *Summa theologiae* I, 12, 7. But see also Eastern theologians, such as John of Damascus, "The Exposition of the Orthodox Faith," in *St. Hilary of Poitiers: Select Works and John of Damascus: Exposition of the Orthodox Faith*, vol. 9 of *A Select Library of Nicene and Post-Nicene Fathers of the Christian Church*, 2nd Ser., ed. Philip Schaff and Henry Wace (Grand Rapids: Eerdmans, 1989), 4, as well as Western Protestants, such as the writers of the Scots Confession of 1560 (chapter 1) and the writers of the Westminster Confession of Faith (chapter 2).

13. See, for example, "Nature and Grace" in *Answer to the Pelagians*, ed. John E. Rotelle, OSA, trans. Roland J. Teske, SJ, vol. I/23, *The Works of Saint Augustine: A Translation for the 21st Century* (Hyde Park, NY: New City Press, 1997), 226–27.

14. Frederick Denison Maurice, *The Kingdom of Christ; or, Hints to a Quaker, Respecting the Principles, Constitution, and Ordinances of the Catholic Church* (London: J. G. F. & J. Rivington, 1842), vol. 1, part 2, ch. 3, 342–78; William J. Wolf, "Introduction" to *An Abridgement of Maurice's Kingdom of Christ* (Lanham, MD: University Press of America, 1983), xxiii.

15. H. Richard Niebuhr, *Christ and Culture* (New York: Harper & Row, 1951), 221.

A further implication is that, as good creatures, humans retain important created capacities, which continue to function and are susceptible to renewal by grace. With respect to knowing God, the world, and ourselves, this means that people have need of special sources as well as the graceful reorientation of their hearts and interests, but also that the created human capacity for reasoning and inquiring after truth has neither been obliterated or erased. The relationship between revelation (or reorienting grace and the historically particular sources of insight in scripture), on the one hand, and our good created human capacity for reasoning and moral responsibility, on the other, is dynamic and complex. It cannot be reduced either to simple equation or opposition.

Human inquiry and reflection therefore are not segregated from revelation and scripture. So, for example, Wesley exhorts "all who seek after true religion to use the reason which God hath given them in searching out the things of God." Indeed, he claims faith is a spiritual sense that discerns God, and that, for those who are given faith and also make use of reason, it is reasonable to love God and neighbor.[16] Again, a number of classical church statements, including the Second Helvetic Confession, make it clear that scripture needs to be interpreted and that human reasoning is deployed as we interpret scripture.[17]

Or again, Thomas Aquinas, Luther, and Calvin all affirm that enough remains of our created gifts—our reasoning capacity and our sense of equity and natural law—to offer guidance in the conduct of life and politics.[18] Calvin also says human competence in

16. See "An Earnest Appeal to Men of Reason and Religion," in *John Wesley*, ed. Albert C. Outler (New York: Oxford University Press, 1964), 386-87, 391, 395.

17. See, for example, the statement about the interpretation of scripture in chapter 2 of the Second Helvetic Confession.

18. Aquinas, *Summa theologiae* I-II, 91, 1-4; I-II, 94, 1-6; Martin Luther, *The Sermon on the Mount (Sermons) and the Magnificat*, ed. Jaroslav Pelikan, vol. 21 of *Luther's Works* (St. Louis: Concordia, 1956), 235-41; *Lectures on Romans: Glosses and Scholia*, ed. Hilton C. Oswald, vol. 25 of *Luther's Works* (St. Louis: Concordia, 1972); "Temporal Authority: To What Extent Should It Be Obeyed?" in *The Christian*

art and science is God's gift, and he maintains that, "if we regard the Spirit of God as the sole fountain of all truth, we shall neither reject the truth itself, nor despise it wherever it shall be found, unless we wish to dishonor the Spirit of God." On this basis, he commends the writings of ancient jurists, philosophers, mathematicians, and physicians. He also claims that those who observe the world with the aid of disciplines such as astronomy, medicine, and natural science behold evidences of God's "wonderful wisdom."[19] Somewhat similarly, Jonathan Edwards ponders, draws, and describes the movements of spiders partly because he regards natural philosophy as the study of the manner of God's acting in the world.[20]

The God of grace disclosed in Jesus Christ stands in relation to persons and to all things as Creator and Redeemer. God's good creation and its orderings reflect divine purposes and care. People are good but also corrupted creatures that stand in need of revelation and regenerating grace. When it comes to true wisdom, or to knowing God, the world, and ourselves in relation, human capacities for reasoning and inquiry are limited and often skewed but also promising. These are some of the signal elements of a pattern of Christian conviction we find in theologians such as Augustine, Aquinas, Luther, Calvin, Wesley, and Maurice, and it is a pattern that furnishes theological reasons for taking seriously the observations and arguments of sciences and other fields of inquiry.[21]

Contemporary theologians who draw on this historic pattern of conviction and adopt collaborative stances work in markedly different ways. An especially important illustration is James M. Gustafson's *Ethics from a Theocentric Perspective*, volume 1, *Theology*

in Society II, ed. Walther I. Brandt, vol. 45 of *Luther's Works* (Philadelphia: Muhlenberg, 1962), 127–29; Calvin, *Institutes*, 2.2.12 (pp. 270–73), 2.2.22–24 (pp. 281–84).

19. Calvin, *Institutes*, 2.2.14–16 (pp. 273–77); 1.5.2 (p. 53).

20. Jonathan Edwards, *Scientific and Philosophical Writings*, ed. Wallace E. Anderson, Works of Jonathan Edwards 6 (New Haven: Yale University Press, 1980), 145–69, 353.

21. A fuller exposition of the pattern would include other elements, such as the relationship between grace or forgiveness and law and between church and world.

and Ethics. Gustafson maintains that theological statements must be in some way congruent with well-attested scientific findings, and this criterion shapes important aspects of his understanding of God and our place in the cosmos.[22] Charles E. Curran's "relationality-responsibility" model in moral theology draws on modern currents in philosophy as well as biblical interpretation and theology. And his view of the human person in terms of multiple relationships with God, world, self, and others is one factor that led him to revise earlier conceptions of natural law and to depart from Catholic teaching on contraception.[23] A collaborative approach is visible in Robin W. Lovin's efforts to revise Christian realism in response to political structures and new realities of our global circumstance interpreted as it is by theologians, philosophers, and political theorists.[24] My own understanding of theological method in *Theology for Liberal Protestants: God the Creator* also reflects a collaborative sensibility.[25]

Consider, too, Philip Clayton's "emergent panentheism." Clayton tries to take into account the concept of emergence—the idea that more complex and even novel dynamic patterns, aggregates, and phenomena emerge from uncorrelated interactions of component parts, and may, in turn, also exert influences on their component parts—as it appears in physical and biological sciences and in philosophy. How, he asks, may Christian theology be reformulated in ways that are responsive to emergentist insights? Or, again, where is a theology of emergence "consistent with traditional theology and

22. Gustafson, *Ethics from a Theocentric Perspective*, vol. 1, *Theology and Ethics*, 252.

23. See Charles E. Curran, *New Look at Christian Morality* (Notre Dame: Fides, 1968), 223–49; *The Catholic Moral Tradition Today: A Synthesis* (Washington, DC: Georgetown University Press, 1999), 60–86; *Loyal Dissent: Memoir of a Catholic Theologian* (Washington, DC: Georgetown University Press, 2006), 79–85.

24. Robin W. Lovin, *Christian Realism and the New Realities* (Cambridge: Cambridge University Press, 2008), 19–42, 117–51.

25. Douglas F. Ottati, *Theology for Liberal Protestants: God the Creator* (Grand Rapids: Eerdmans, 2013), 9, 25–34, 135–48.

where do the two diverge?"[26] Thus, while Clayton believes "the theistic worldview" of the Abrahamic traditions portrays "the amazing fecundity of natural evolution" as expressive of "the intentional creative structuring of God," he also accepts that the idea of emergence undercuts some traditional understandings of the deity.[27]

William Schweiker's "theological humanism," a stance that faces "the unhappiness, poverty, pettiness, and violence of human beings, but does not believe that those facts are the truth of life," places considerable weight not only on biblical texts and the insights of classical and recent theologians, but also on the contributions of philosophy and the humanities.[28] For Schweiker, our contemporary age is one characterized by a radical extension of human power that "blunts our sensibility to the ubiquity of value in the world and endangers human life"—a reading that draws on philosophers like Hans Jonas and Erazim Kohak, and poets like Czeslaw Milosz.[29] He also develops his original interpretation of human agency—we are bound by impulses to self-love and domination but also the constraints and direction of the moral law and its imperative to respect and enhance the integrity of life with and for others—in sustained conversation with Kant's philosophy and its more recent interpreters such as Emmanuel Levinas.[30]

---

26. Philip Clayton, "Toward a Constructive Christian Theology of Emergence," in *Evolution and Emergence: Systems, Organisms, Persons*, ed. Nancey Murphy and William R. Stoeger, SJ (Oxford: Oxford University Press, 2007), 315. The essay also outlines how Clayton would treat eight traditional and systematic loci of Christian theology.

27. Philip Clayton, "Emergence from Quantum Physics to Religion," in *The Re-Emergence of Emergence: The Emergentist Hypothesis from Science to Religion*, ed. Philip Clayton and Paul Davies (Oxford: Oxford University Press, 2006), 319–20.

28. William Schweiker, *Theological Ethics and Global Dynamics: In the Time of Many Worlds* (Oxford: Blackwell, 2004), 215–16.

29. William Schweiker, *Dust That Breathes: Christian Faith and the New Humanisms* (Oxford: Wiley-Blackwell, 2010), 88.

30. William Schweiker, "The Love of Power," in *Renegotiating Power, Theology, and Politics*, ed. Joshua Daniel and Rick Elgendy (New York: Palgrave Macmillan, 2015), 19–20.

This is not to deny that theologians who draw on the historic pattern visible in Augustine, Luther, Wesley, and the rest sometimes entertain significant disagreements. Theologians who work with different Christian subtraditions, e.g., Roman Catholic, Lutheran, Reformed, and Methodist, typically understand certain doctrines differently, e.g., incarnation, sin, justification, sanctification, law, and church. An especially important difference for our purposes here concerns the authority of church teaching and openness to revision. Some Roman Catholics are comfortable talking about revising interpretations of doctrines but not revising the doctrines themselves, whereas some liberal Protestants are willing to speak of both. Time and again—for example, with respect to the place of Earth in our solar system, evolution versus Genesis, and human sexuality—ecclesiastical trials and censures, both Catholic and Protestant, have moved to impose limits on collaboration that proved in the end to be untenable. The way in which a theologian resolves this issue and negotiates these impositions influences whether and how she or he will inhabit the tension between openness to revisions and maintaining the integrity of specifically Christian wisdom.

Prominent Alternatives

To see how the collaborative manner of theologizing I advocate differs from some contemporary alternatives, return for a moment to the period of disciplinary differentiation, which allowed for disagreement and debate within a single discipline while also insulating each discipline from external standards of judgment. What is now clear is that in many ways Christian theologians adapted themselves to the modern intellectual climate of discrete disciplinary thinking.

Consider Karl Barth's understanding of dogmatics as the "self-examination of the Christian church with respect to the content of its distinctive talk about God."[31] On the one hand, he questions whether Christian theology should be confined within the boundaries of a discipline at all, and he clearly refuses to relinquish Christian theology's panoramic intent with respect to picturing human life *coram Deo*. Nevertheless, Barth is also adamant that, as the church's distinctive talk, theology's sole criterion or principle is the being of God in Jesus Christ, the Word of God, or revelation in Jesus Christ alone, and that theology must not be deflected by "alien principles." Theology's criticism and correction of talk about God proceeds "according to the criterion of the Church's own principle."[32] And indeed, "if theology allows itself to be called, or calls itself, a science, it cannot in doing so accept the obligation of submission to standards valid for other sciences."[33] Somewhat paradoxically, then, Barth's insistence on revelation alone—an insistence which, in the eyes of many, resists accommodation to modernity—not only distinguishes his inquiry and its logic or rationality from other inquiries, but may also be seen in part as a theological capitulation to the modern intellectual climate of discrete disciplinary thinking.

George Lindbeck's postliberal theology leads to similarly insulating results. Christianity, says Lindbeck, is a cultural-linguistic system that rests on the biblical narrative and furnishes an incommensurable and untranslatable interpretative framework within which believers live their lives and understand reality.[34] A major responsibility of Christian theology therefore is to display or enact the interpretation of the world inherent in the Christian framework. The circle is not entirely closed; theology also works with the Christian interpretative framework to assimilate the changing and varied situations and realities Christians encounter at various places and times by furnishing intelligible interpretations of them in its own

31. Karl Barth, *Church Dogmatics* I/1:3.

32. CD I/1:6, 15, 47–87.

33. CD I/1:10.

34. George A. Lindbeck, *The Nature of Doctrine: Religion and Theology in a Postliberal Age* (Philadelphia: Westminster, 1984), 117, 134.

terms. Lindbeck calls this "intelligibility as skill," and it points to the history of reasoning internal to theology. That is, theology shows adherents how the terms of the Christian interpretative framework make sense of the postbiblical situations and realities they encounter. But nowhere does Lindbeck explore the possibility a collaborative manner of theologizing cannot dismiss, namely, that elements of the Christian interpretative framework itself might need to be revised as we interpret and assimilate situations and realities, e.g., human sexuality, natural ecosystems, that are also interpreted by other disciplines, e.g., evolutionary biology and environmental studies, which deploy additional interpretative frameworks.

Barth's revelational insularity and the asymmetry of Lindbeck's proposal to absorb the world into the incommensurable grammar and terms of the biblical text are present also in the work of some contemporary neo–Radical Reformation theologians who resonate with a different historic pattern of Christian conviction from the one I described earlier. A primary conviction here is that the Christian community must remain loyal to Jesus Christ rather than compromise with a fallen world. So, for example, the sixteenth-century Reformer Menno Simons regards the church as a holy community set apart from a world in which people live in "mighty opposition to all that God teaches and commands" and "the voice of the devil is everywhere."[35] Peter Rideman's claim that civil government "has its place outside Christ but not in Christ" emphasizes a similar conflict between Christ's rule in the church and the reign of fallen principalities and powers.[36] Thus, rather than discuss a created capacity for reasoning or a sense of equity that continues to function and to offer guidance, these radical Reformers emphasize strict discipleship. True faithfulness is the commitment to follow the way of God's Word in Jesus Christ rather than other (and alien) lords.

35. *The Complete Writings of Menno Simons* (Scottdale, PA: Herald, 1956), 111, 180–81, 232.

36. Peter Rideman, *Account of Our Religion, Doctrine and Faith* (Rifton, NY: Plough Publishing House, 1970), 107, 108, 111–14, 105.

John Howard Yoder's striking articulation of a neo–Radical Reformation stance stresses that Jesus brings a way or direction in living that founds the church and that contrasts with fallen principalities and powers.[37] But it is no mere repetition of sixteenth-century theologizing; Yoder joins this affirmation with something like Barth's insulating insistence that theology not accommodate itself to alien standards of meaning and truth. Its sole criterion or principle is the revealed Word in Jesus Christ.[38]

Stanley Hauerwas, whose thinking is influenced by Yoder's achievement, regards Barth as a hero of modern theology precisely because Barth refuses to accommodate Christian theology to alien sources and standards.[39] Hauerwas claims Jesus is the *autobasileia*, the reign or kingdom of God in person, and that "Jesus is the story that forms the church" as a kind of "contrast model" to the world.[40] Thus, the church is "the only true polity we can know in this life."[41] It is "a colony" that rejects the dominant culture with a few exceptions, and that forms Christians as resident aliens, "a beachhead, an outpost, and island of one culture in the middle of another."[42]

With respect to sources of insight, Hauerwas asserts (like Lindbeck) that human rationality and truth claims are inelucta-

37. John Howard Yoder, *The Original Revolution: Essays on Christian Pacifism* (Scottdale, PA: Herald, 1977), 13–33; *The Politics of Jesus: Vicit Agnus Noster*, 2nd ed. (Grand Rapids: Eerdmans, 1994), 112–33.

38. See Stanley Hauerwas, *With the Grain of the Universe* (Grand Rapids: Brazos, 2001), 216–25.

39. Hauerwas, *With the Grain of the Universe*, 206.

40. Stanley Hauerwas, *A Community of Character: Toward a Constructive Christian Social Ethic* (Notre Dame: University of Notre Dame Press, 1981), 45, 50–51.

41. Stanley Hauerwas, *Against the Nations: War and Survival in a Liberal Society* (Minneapolis: Winston, 1985), 130. Hauerwas distinguishes his position from "the Anabaptist vision" but also claims to be "a high church Mennonite." See Hauerwas, *In Good Company: The Church as Polis* (Notre Dame: University of Notre Dame Press, 1995), 62, 65–78.

42. Stanley Hauerwas and William H. Willimon, *Resident Aliens: Life in the Christian Colony* (Nashville: Abingdon Press, 1989), 12, 44–47.

bly narrative-dependent.[43] There is, then, no more or less common human reasoning or rationality that different communities may deploy, and there are no impartial criteria for judging among the stories that lend coherence to our lives.[44] The church, like all other communities, accepts "a certain set of stories as canonical." Its most important task is "to be a community capable of hearing the story of God we find in scripture and living in a manner that is faithful to that story."[45] Furthermore, "there is no standpoint external to the practice of Christianity for assessing the truth of Christian convictions," and it is a mistake to attempt to translate the language of the Christian community into other terms.[46]

Differences between the collaborative theological stance that I am advocating here and the neo–Radical Reformation theologians run deep. For example, I think both Yoder and Hauerwas finally insulate Christian theology and ethics in a manner reminiscent of the rise of the modern discrete disciplines, and I wonder whether this might not count as a kind of accommodation to the culture. I also think neo–Radical Reformation stances affirm a kind of restricted presence of God in Christ without a discernible divine government in the world beyond the church. Their theological reasons for doing so include the affirmation that sin infects the world considerably more virulently than the holy community called church. But the basic theological question this raises is whether the Radical Reformation pattern finally does justice to the conviction that God creates and redeems the world. Might a more robust affirmation of God as the Creator and Redeemer of all things dispose theologians more favorably toward the possibility that our conversations with those who utilize different interpretative frameworks may sometimes help

43. Stanley Hauerwas and L. Gregory Jones, *Why Narrative? Readings in Narrative Theology* (Grand Rapids: Eerdmans, 1989), 4, 12, 169.

44. Hauerwas and Jones, *Why Narrative?*, 185, 190.

45. Hauerwas and Jones, *Why Narrative?*, 190; Hauerwas, *A Community of Character*, 1.

46. Hauerwas, *With the Grain of the Universe*, 222, 231.

to improve and correct our own theology and ethics?[47] Thus, in my view, a related question concerns the kinds of conversations Christian theologians are likely to have with representatives of other disciplines and inquiries. Other than telling the modern disciplines that their frameworks are themselves narratively dependent, not neutral, and, in a Christian context, often pernicious, is there really anything else left for the neo–Radical Reformation theologians to say?

Consider the contemporary theological movement called Radical Orthodoxy. It is sufficiently fluid, ecumenical, and even "fuzzy" to discourage one from identifying it too closely with a specific pattern of basic Christian convictions.[48] John Milbank, its most important representative, criticizes Barth for not escaping "a hidden negative determination of what revelation must mean" according to a "seemingly abandoned" post-Kantian "extrinsicist framework."[49] At the same time, he argues that Lindbeck and Hans Frei are correct to call us back to narrative, but that, if we pay greater attention to the complexities of the biblical narrative, we shall also see that "it always in a fashion anticipates the speculative task of ontology and theology."[50] Indeed, "the paradigmatic dimension of narrative shows that an ontological questioning is 'always already begun,'" and that there is an ontology implicit in scripture that makes sweeping claims.[51]

47. But, of course, I am also bound to add that the difference appears equally serious when viewed from the other side. For the neo–Radical Reformation theologians, those of us disposed to enter into collaborative conversations with representatives of other disciplines and inquiries jeopardize the integrity of the scriptural story and its integral formation of faithful witnesses.

48. John Milbank, "The Grandeur of Reason and the Perversity of Rationalism: Radical Orthodoxy's First Decade," in *The Radical Orthodoxy Reader*, ed. John Milbank and Simon Oliver (London: Routledge, 2009), 367.

49. Milbank, "The Grandeur of Reason and the Perversity of Rationalism," in *The Radical Orthodoxy Reader*, 368.

50. John Milbank, *Theology and Social Theory: Beyond Secular Reason*, 2nd ed. (Oxford: Blackwell, 1990, 2006), 387.

51. Milbank, *Theology and Social Theory*, 390.

Accordingly, Milbank and other radically orthodox thinkers appreciate that Christian theology cannot be "just like another discipline alongside others."[52] They retain the sense that Christian theology—as in its classical medieval forms—seeks a comprehensive vision that does not have a sharply delineated subject matter. Indeed, Simon Oliver describes the subject matter of theology in much the same way I did earlier in this essay—"God and all things in relation to God." This is what distinguishes theology from disciplines with clearly limited and mutually exclusive purviews. Moreover, says Oliver, theology, as Radical Orthodoxy conceives of it, does not stand in isolation from other inquiries, but "is in constant critical engagement with other disciplines."[53]

This is so because a central element of their stance is a "participatory ontology," in which God is being itself and all other things have their existence by participation. Thus, in a manner that makes explicit what is already begun in the biblical narrative, being is seen to include both world and God, both nature and supernature. Reality cannot be reduced to nature alone; neither can nature and supernature be separated. The natural is indissolubly and dependently connected with the supernatural, and, much like an icon, nature points beyond itself to God or to being itself.

Historically this Christian ontology meets a serious challenge in ideas, themes, and arguments that reach epochal expression in Duns Scotus. The key secular idea is *natura pura*, or the idea that autonomous nature alone is all there is. This idea, in turn, gives rise to the modern autonomous disciplines that claim to be neutral and self-contained statements about purely natural reality. But what all this masks, says Milbank, is that the idea of *natura pura* is not the end of metaphysics; it is only a different, secular metaphysics of autonomy in which we no longer understand either ourselves or

52. Simon Oliver, "Introducing Radical Orthodoxy," in *The Radical Orthodoxy Reader*, 20–21.
53. Oliver, "Introducing Radical Orthodoxy," 19–20.

our world to participate in a larger realm of being, its structures and direction.[54]

Thus, when representatives of allegedly autonomous disciplines present their interpretations of human life and the world apart from any transcendent reference they are not neutral. They are in fact propounding views that only make sense apart from the true Christian metaphysics. And, since there is no universal foundational point from which to judge the different metaphysics, the one thing a Christian theologian needs to emphasize is simply that there is nothing necessary or objective about the assumptions within which the secular disciplines operate. Indeed, from a perspective defined by theological and ontological statements generated from within the Christian narrative, representatives of the allegedly autonomous disciplines are really just doing bad theology.

Consider the purportedly neutral social scientific interpretations of human societies and the many different forms of life these societies engender and support. The problem according to Milbank is that, having exchanged a participatory metaphysics for one that celebrates simple autonomy, the social sciences fail to read and to analyze the many societies in light of the true Christian ontology and its claim that the church itself exhibits the exemplary form of human community in connection with transcendent reality.[55] Instead, they try to regard all societies and forms of life on a par because they "nihilistically" attempt to understand the world apart from any reference to transcendent reality. The theologian therefore dismisses the social sciences, and calls for a "Christian sociology" that draws on a speculative ontology grounded in the scriptural narrative.

The result, says Milbank, is that theology itself becomes a kind of sociology that supports a Christian counter-history of human associations, something like his reading of Augustine's *City of God*.

54. Milbank, "The Grandeur of Reason and the Perversity of Rationalism," 373–74.
55. Milbank, *Theology and Social Theory*, 389.

It relocates all political theory in relation to the church. And it commends a counter-ethics, which promotes charity and forgiveness as appropriate to an existence that is gratuitously given, the fulfilling of true virtue through reconciliation, and the primary reality of peace rather than violence.[56]

The theological stance I advocate differs sharply from all of this, and prompts one to raise certain questions. Should we claim that there is a single Christian ontology or that the Bible favors one ontology above all others? (Tillichians and process theologians will no doubt raise similar questions.)[57] Indeed, why should we favor the participatory metaphysics that Milbank commends? A Thomist of a different sort might say that the metaphysics should be preferred because it's true, or because one may marshal more general reasons and arguments in its favor, some of which might draw on the findings of nontheological scholarship. Partly because of their conviction that all truth claims are narrative-dependent, Radical Orthodox theologians make no such arguments. They are satisfied instead with (a) pointing out that the allegedly autonomous disciplines presuppose an ontological claim, i.e., that *natura pura* is the whole of reality, which these disciplines fail to acknowledge, and (b) choosing to work instead with the participatory "Christian" ontology.

Additional questions concern the way in which theologians engage other disciplines and inquiries. It is true that, after a fashion, Radical Orthodox theologians engage other disciplines. Their ontology requires that they do so. But one wonders whether they can move beyond a critical dismissal of other disciplines as bad theology. Can they enter into the sorts of discussions and exchanges that may lead them toward transdisciplinary learning and revision of their theology? Perhaps, though it seems entirely possible that the critique of secular autonomy based in its "untouchable" on-

56. Milbank, *Theology and Social Theory*, 410, 429.
57. See, for example, Lewis S. Ford, *The Lure of God: A Biblical Background for Process Theism* (Philadelphia: Fortress, 1978).

158

tology will insulate Radical Orthodoxy from all findings of other disciplines. There are reasons to think Radical Orthodoxy is not merely a neo-scholastic repristination of classical medieval thinking (among them the sheer fluidity and diversity of the movement and the fact that more traditional Thomists will be uncomfortable with the affirmation of the radical narrative dependency of theology, ontology, and all claims to truth). The question remains: Does Radical Orthodoxy accord overly much authority to a particular reading of medieval Christian ontology and thus, in effect, mimic a signal feature of the modern insular disciplines?

Conclusion

Can a collaborative manner of theologizing produce significant results for contemporary Christian theology and the church? I think so, especially in settings where sustained conversations with those who work in other disciplines are valued and supported. Indeed, the relevance of a collaborative stance should be plain to those who stand in Roman Catholic, Anglican, Lutheran, Reformed, and Methodist theological traditions that see the intellectual importance of taking into account circumstances and realities that secular sciences and philosophers account for naturalistically. Moreover, since everyone in a modern Western culture such as our own—and not only the highly educated—is exposed to multiple interpretations of actions, events, texts, etc., a sense for how nonreligious accounts affect theological and religious ones is important for preaching, teaching, and pastoral care.[58] Pastors and preachers in very many contexts would therefore do well to proceed with something like a collaborative sensibility.

I close simply by repeating four theses. (1) Conversations like

58. James M. Gustafson makes these last two points in *An Examined Faith: The Grace of Self-Doubt* (Minneapolis: Fortress, 2004), 6-9.

those at the Center of Theological Inquiry and elsewhere reflect a multidisciplinary intellectual milieu in which the limitations of insular disciplinary thinking are increasingly recognized. (2) Sustained participation in these conversations presents Christian theologians, whose field of inquiry never was entirely like the modern disciplines, with considerable opportunities, while also requiring them to inhabit the tension between openness to revision and maintaining the integrity of Christian wisdom. (3) A particular historic pattern of Christian convictions lends considerable support to a collaborative stance that pursues these opportunities and is alert to this tension. And, (4) this theological stance differs sharply from some rather prominent contemporary alternatives. May those theologians and ministers who take it up increase in number and in strength.

Contributors

John P. Burgess is James Henry Snowden Professor of Systematic Theology at Pittsburgh Theological Seminary. He was a research fellow in the Inquiry on Law and Religious Freedom.

Peter Danchin is professor of law and co-director of the International and Comparative Law Program at the University of Maryland School of Law. He was a senior research fellow in the Inquiry on Law and Religious Freedom.

Celia Deane-Drummond is professor of theology at the University of Notre Dame. She was a senior research fellow in the Inquiry on Evolution and Human Nature.

Agustín Fuentes is professor of anthropology at the University of Notre Dame. He was a research fellow in the Inquiry on Evolution and Human Nature.

Andrea Hollingsworth is adjunct professor of theology at United Theological Seminary of the Twin Cities. She was a research fellow in the Inquiry on Religious Experience and Moral Identity.

Robin W. Lovin is William H. Scheide Senior Fellow in Theology at the Center of Theological Inquiry. He was project leader for the three-year New Approaches in Theological Inquiry project.

Joshua Mauldin is outreach officer at the Center of Theological Inquiry. He was a research fellow in the Inquiry on Law and Religious Freedom.

Friederike Nüssel is professor of systematic theology and director of the Ecumenical Institute at the University of Heidelberg. She was project co-leader for the three-year New Approaches in Theological Inquiry project.

Mary Ellen O'Connell is Robert and Marion Short Professor of Law at the University of Notre Dame. She was a senior research fellow in the Inquiry on Law and Religious Freedom.

Douglas F. Ottati is Craig Family Distinguished Professor of Reformed Theology and Justice at Davidson College.

Stephen Pope is professor of theology at Boston College. He was a senior research fellow in the Inquiry on Religious Experience and Moral Identity.

Colleen Shantz is associate professor of New Testament studies at St. Michael's College in the University of Toronto. She was a research fellow in the Inquiry on Religious Experience and Moral Identity.

Michael Spezio is associate professor of psychology at Scripps College. He was a research fellow in the Inquiry on Religious Experience and Moral Identity.

Center of Theological Inquiry Research Fellows, 2012–2015

Inquiry on Evolution and Human Nature

Lee Cronk

Conor Cunningham

Celia Deane-Drummond

Agustín Fuentes

Jan-Olav Henriksen

Nicola Hoggard-Creegan

Dominic Johnson

Hillary Lenfesty

Markus Mühling

Eugene Rogers

Jeffrey Schloss

Robert Song

Richard Sosis

Aku Visala

Inquiry on Religious Experience and Moral Identity

Gordon Burghardt

George Graham

Andrea Hollingsworth

Brick Johnstone

Friederike Nüssel

Sheryl Overmyer
Stephen Pope
Arne Rasmussen
Robert Roberts
Colleen Shantz
Michael Spezio
Wesley Wildman

Inquiry on Law and Religious Freedom

John Burgess
Peter Danchin
David Decosimo
Silvio Ferrari
Gábor Halmai
Stacy Johnson
Robin Lovin
Jessica Lowe
Joshua Mauldin
Mark Modak-Truran
Mary Ellen O'Connell
Hans-Martien ten Napel
Zhibin Xie

Index

Aesthetics, 113–14, 118–20
Albo, Joseph, 6
Alfsvåg, Knut, 89
Allott, Philip, 128
Arendt, Hannah, 121–23, 126
Aristotle, 125, 127
Augustine, 127, 140, 145, 147, 150, 157; *City of God,* 140, 157

Baidou, Alain, 62
Barth, Karl, xxx, 30–31, 34, 150–51, 152, 153, 155
Batozskii, Tavrion, 107
Benton Facial Recognition Task, 28
Bethge, Eberhard, 40–42
Bolshevik(s), 93, 94, 98, 101, 102–4, 106–7
Bond, H. Lawrence, 71
Bonhoeffer, Dietrich, 40–42, 43
Boyle, Gregory, 38–40, 43

Calvin, John, 137, 144, 146–47
Canuel, Mark, 123, 128–29
Castelli, Elizabeth, 106
Centering Prayer, 32–33
Certeau, Michel de, 76
Cessario, Romanus, 45
Christian realism, 148
Clayton, Philip, 148–49
Coakley, Sarah, 16
Cognition: cognitive averaging, 27;

cognitive ecology, 52. *See also* Embodied cognition
Collaborative sensibility, 133–35, 143, 148
Confessors (Russian Orthodoxy), 96, 97
Continental and analytic philosophy, 12–13
Conversion (vs. religious experience), 52–54
Curran, Charles E., 148

Dalai Lama, 32
Damasio, Antonio, 56
Dante, 127
Deane-Drummond, Celia, 51
Decentering, 69, 75–77
Derrida, Jacques, 13
Diedrich, Hans-Christian, 105
Donskoi, Dmitrii, 104
Douzinas, Costas, 129
Dual-process theory, 54–55
Duns Scotus, 156–58

Eagleton, Terry, 122
Early hominin evolution, 7
Early human origins, 1–2, 4, 12
Ecstatic experience, 61–62
Edwards, Jonathan, 147
Embodied cognition, 55
Emergent panentheism, 148–49

Ethology, 26

Evolutionary science: contemporary, 10; evolutionary anthropology, 1, 2, 17, 18, 21; evolutionary biology, 2, 10, 14, 20, 21; evolutionary psychology, 17; evolutionary theory, 4, 10, 65–67

Evolutionary theism, 10. *See also* Teleology, vs. evolutionary theory

Exemplar paradox, 32

Exemplars: communities or persons, 32–33, 37; moral, 26, 30, 32, 35

Flourishing, 27

Formalism, legal, 117

Forte, Bruno, 130

Foundationalism (epistemology), 8–9

Francis (pope), 10, 11

Freedom. *See* Spiritual vs. religious freedom

Frei, Hans, 155

Genesis, biblical creation accounts in, 2, 4, 6, 10, 52

Gorbachev, Mikhail, 95; *glasnost*, 95; *perestroika*, 95

Grace, as beginning of moral life, 30, 37, 40

Graham, Gordon, 119

Grammar (theological), xxiv, xxvi

Grotius, Hugo, 115, 129

Grünewald, Matthias, 34

Gustafson, James M., 137, 147–48

Habitus, 24, 26, 34, 37, 40, 43; habit vs. *habitus*, 44–49

Haidt, Jonathan, 61–62

Haig, David, 58

Hart, H. L. A., 114, 118

Hauerwas, Stanley, 153–54

Herdt, Jennifer, 48

Hoff, Johannes, 87

Holy elders (*startsy*), 99, 104, 107, 109

Holy fool (Russian Orthodoxy), 100

Homeboy Industries, 37–39

Homo economicus / homo rationalis, 35

Human nature, 5–6

Hume, David, 124–26; pleasure principle, 124

Humility and hope (interdisciplinary virtues), xxix–xxxiii, 111, 141–43

Imago Dei, 51, 52, 64–67

Imitatio, 24, 26, 34, 37, 38–39, 42–43, 48

Integration, 69, 84–89

Isenheim Altarpiece, 34

James, William, 46

John Paul II (pope), 10

Jonas, Hans, 149

Jubilee Bishops Council (Russian Orthodoxy), 96

Kahneman, Daniel, 54, 56, 64

Kant, Immanuel, 120–21, 122, 123, 125, 126, 149

Keating, Thomas, 32

Keltner, Dacher, 61–62

Khrushchev, Nikita, 95

Kierkegaard, Søren, 130

Kirill (patriarch), 108

Kohak, Erazim, 149

L'Arche (community), 33, 37

Laudato Si', 11

Legal authority, 113

Legal science, 116–17

Levinas, Emmanuel, 149

Lindbeck, George, 151–52, 153, 155

Lovin, Robin, 148; Christian realism, 148

Luther, Martin, 144, 146, 147, 150

Mahoney, Jack, 10, 12
Maurice, F. D., 144, 145, 147
Mazyrin, Aleksandr, 104
McGinn, Bernard, 71
McKenny, Gerald, 30–31
McNamara, Patrick, 69, 74, 75, 81, 82, 84–85, 88
Meaning-maintenance theory, 54
Milbank, John, 155, 156, 157
Milosz, Czeslaw, 149
Mittleman, Alan, 2, 4, 5, 11
Model-based learning, 48–49
Moral averaging, 29–30
Moral theology, 148
Moral transformation, 36, 37
Moss, Candida, 106
Murdoch, Iris, 120, 124, 126, 127

Natural law, 148
Natural selection, 19, 20
Natural theology, xxiv, xxvii, 16
Neale, David T., 96
Neo–Radical Reformation, 152–54
Nevskii, Alexander, 104
Newman, Barbara, 73
New martyrs (Russian Orthodoxy), 93, 96, 97, 98, 101, 103–4, 107, 109
Niche construction, 2, 18–19
Nicholas II (czar), 97
Nicholas of Cusa, 68–90; *admiratio*, 72, 75, 76, 79; *caritas, amor*, 72; *coincidentia oppositorum*, 76, 82, 83, 85; deification (*theōsis*), 69, 71; *De visione Dei*, 68–70, 71–72, 76–85, 87–90; *filiatio / Christi-formitas*, 85; *imitatio Christi*, 87; learned ignorance, 79, 81, 83; providence, 79, 81, 83; simulation, 85; transformation-of-self, 69, 73,

74, 75; union with God, 69; *visio Dei*, 71
Niebuhr, H. Richard, 137
Nietzsche, Friedrich, 130
Novak, David, 125–26
Nowak, Martin, 16

October Revolution (Russia), 94
Oliver, Simon, 156
Original sin, 10, 12
Ottati, Douglas, 148

Parallel-process theory, 54
Passion-bearers (Russian Orthodoxy), 96, 97
Paul (apostle), 50, 52–54, 60, 63, 64
Pinckaers, Servais, 44
Plato, 125, 127
Polianskii, Petr, 104
Poor, Sara, 73
Postfoundationalism (epistemology), 8, 14
Primordial history, 3–4
Proulx, Travis, 58–60

Radical Orthodoxy, 155, 156, 158–59
Rahner, Karl, 2, 3, 7, 12
Rawls, John, 123
Reappraisal, 69, 81–84
Reddy, Vasudevi, 77
Reformed theological ethics, 30–31
Religious experience, 50, 53–54, 60–61
Renovationists (Russian Orthodoxy), 98
Reynhout, Ken, 13, 14
Ricoeur, Paul, 13–14
Rideman, Peter, 152
Rupture-repair, 69, 77–80, 81

Saint-consciousness, 38, 41
Scarry, Elaine, 126–27
Schloss, Jeff, 17

Schweiker, William, 149
Scientific realism, xxiv
Scots Confession (1560), 144–45
Second Helvetic Confession, 146
Simons, Menno, 152
Skepticism, xvii
Smith, Stephen, 117, 118
Sovereignty, 116
Spezio, Michael L., 88
Spiritual vs. religious freedom, 109–11
Stalin's Great Terror, 95
Stang, Charles M., 73

Teleology, vs. evolutionary theory, 65–67
Theo-drama, 2, 18, 20, 21
Theological humanism, 149
Theological realism, xxiii–xxvii, xxviii
Thomas à Kempis, 40–41
Thomas Aquinas, 43, 44, 51, 75, 125, 127, 137, 144, 146, 147
Tikhon (patriarch), 98, 104, 107
Torrell, Jean-Pierre, 44–45
Transdisciplinarity, xxiii, 2, 14, 16, 18, 134, 143
Transversal approach, 12; transversal reasoning, 8; transversal space, 2, 7, 12, 13
Troeltsch, Ernst, 105
Troitskii, Pavel, 100
Tuchkov, Evgenii, 104

Van Huyssteen, Wentzel, 2, 7, 12, 14, 16
Vanier, Jean, 33, 37
Varela, Francisco, 25
Vasil'ev, Ioann, 102
Vattel, Emmerich de, 116
Virtue science, 24, 34
Virtue theory, 30–31
Von Balthasar, Hans Urs, 20, 130
Vorob'ev, Vladimir, 105, 107

Weil, Simone, 127
Wesley, John, 144, 146, 147, 150
Westminster Confession of Faith (1647), 144–45
Wood, Wendy, 46

Yoder, John Howard, 153, 154

Zagzebski, Linda, 29
Ziebart, K. M., 76